Elections

After an introductory chapter concerned with a discussion of democratic theory, Eckhard Jesse's new book provides a first-class survey of elections and electoral laws in the Federal Republic. His lucid analysis is packed with detailed information, including data on the sociology of the German electorate. Above all, by treating the topic against the background of the French and British electoral systems, the author adds a genuinely comparative dimension which greatly enhances our understanding of the peculiarities of the West German situation. Complemented by some 15 statistical tables, this study will be indispensable to all interested in modern German politics at a regional, national and European Community level.

Eckhard Jesse is Associate Professor in the Department of Political Science, University of Trier.

GERMAN STUDIES SERIES

Elections

The Federal Republic of Germany in Comparison

Eckhard Jesse

JN
3971
.A95
J47
1990
West

Translated from the German by
Lindsay Batson

BERG

New York / Oxford / Munich

Distributed exclusively in the US and Canada by
St. Martin's Press, New York

This enlarged and updated English edition
first published in 1990 by
Berg Publishers Limited
Editorial Offices:
165 Taber Avenue, Providence, R.I., 02906, USA
150 Cowley Road, Oxford OX4 1JJ, UK
Westermühlstraße 26, 8000 München 5, FRG

© Berg Publishers Limited 1990

German edition, *Wahlen: Bundesrepublik Deutschland im Vergleich*,
first published by Colloquium Verlag, Berlin
© Colloquium Verlag, 1988

Library of Congress Cataloging-in-Publication Data
Jesse, Eckhard, 1948-
[Wahlen. English]
Elections : the Federal Republic of Germany in comparison /
Eckhard Jesse : translated from the German by Lindsay Batson.
p. cm. — (German studies series)
Translation of: Wahlen.
Includes bibliographical references.
ISBN 0–85496–647–1
1. Elections—Germany (West) 2. Elections—Europe.
3. Comparative government. I. Title. II. Series.
JN3971.A95J47 1990   90–355
324.6'0943—dc20   CIP

British Library Cataloguing in Publication Data
Jesse, Eckhard
Elections : the Federal Republic of Germany in comparison.
– (German studies series).
1. West Germany. Federal elections
I. Title II. Series III. Wahlen. *English*
324.943
ISBN 0–85496–647–1

Printed in Great Britain by Billing and Sons Ltd, Worcester

Contents

List of Tables and Figures

Tables

Figure

Introduction: Structure and Contents

'In order to evaluate a political system, one must primarily question the real meaning of the elections practised in this system.'[1] The way in which elections are carried out and the form that they take are decisive for the classification of systems of rule. It is not surprising, then, that both Karl Loewenstein in his book *Verfassungslehre* and Robert A. Dahl in *Die politische Analyse* pay considerable attention to the role of elections when classifying systems of rule.[2] In democracies, elections are the definitive legitimising mechanism of the political system. They determine who is to be granted political responsibility for the community for a fixed period of time. As such, they receive a good deal of attention, both from politicians and from the electorate and public opinion, and, not least, from certain social sciences, such as political science and sociology.

This volume is divided into three main chapters (2–4). In Chapter 2 ('Elections and Democracy'), the theoretical aspects of democracy and the question of how democratic elections differ from non-democratic elections are the main subjects covered, together with the criticisms levelled at elections from various, if not opposing, points of view. Chapter 3 considers the role of elections and electoral systems in the United Kingdom, France and Germany. These three countries lend themselves to comparison, on the one hand because of their different patterns of political development and, on the other, because their electoral systems have different characteristics. At the same time, there has been a certain convergence in voting-behaviour towards bipolarity. Chapter 4 considers the complex subject of elections and voting-rights in West Germany, and pays equal attention to voting-structure and the sociology of elections.

1. Heiner Flohr, *Rationalität und Politik*, vol. 2, Neuwied and Berlin, 1975, p. 61.
2. See Karl Loewenstein, *Verfassungslehre* (1957), 3rd edn, Tübingen, 1975, p. 275; Robert A. Dahl, *Die politische Analyse* (1963), Munich, 1973, p. 106f.

1

The general question which is to be considered is the extent to which elections are an essential, integral part of maintaining and further developing democracy. What is the relationship between the identity and the competitive theories of democracy and elections? What does the much-emphasised 'freedom of elections' entail? How do the rules on voting-rights differ from country to country? Should the electoral system in West Germany be changed? What factors influence voting-behaviour? Are there any alternatives to elections which could be considered adequate from a democratic point of view? These are just a few of the questions which must be answered.

But first it is worth considering briefly the current level of research. This is necessary because the presentation of problems in this book is concise. How are elections and electoral systems analysed and assessed in the scientific literature? What has been achieved in the field of comparative international studies? Has there been any attempt to connect West German electoral research with similar studies in other countries? In which areas is there a lot of material available, and where are there considerable research gaps? These questions form the basis of Chapter 1.

1
The State of Research

As elections are the most important mechanism by which democracies secure their legitimacy, they are one of the main fields of research in political science, as is shown by the numerous publications that discuss them.[1] Of course, there is particular emphasis on certain areas, notably the sociology of voting and research into electoral systems. These two areas will be treated separately in the chapter focusing on elections in West Germany (Chapter 4).

Up to now, researchers have paid comparatively little attention to the admittedly heterogeneous subject discussed in Chapter 2 of this book: the relationship between elections and democracy, the study of which combines theory and history. Dolf Sternberger, one of the 'old masters' of German political science, has in numerous publications expressed his opinions on the extent to which elections are connected with the political legitimacy of a democratic system.[2] Due in particular to the considerable legitimising-powers which elections have, few dictatorships are able to avoid them. This complex area[3] has

---

1. See for example Rainer-Olaf Schultze, 'Neuere Literatur zur Wahl im Überblick', *Politische Vierteljahresschrift*, 18/1977, pp. 689–704; Peter Steinbach, 'Stand und Methode des historischen Wahlforschung', in Hartmut Kaelble (ed.), *Probleme der Modernisierung in Deutschland. Sozialhistorische Studien zum 19. und 20. Jahrhundert*, Opladen, 1978, pp. 171–234; Arend Lijphart, 'The Field of Electoral Systems Research: A Critical Survey', *Electoral Studies*, 4/1985, pp. 3–14; Eckhard Jesse, 'Wahlen in der Bundesrepublik Deutschland und anderswo', in Eckhard Jesse, *Literaturführer: Parlamentarische Demokratie*, Opladen, 1981, pp. 171–208; Eckhard Jesse, 'Internationale Wahlsystemforschung: Probleme und Perspektiven', *PVS-Literatur*, 27/1986, pp. 157–67; Eckhard Jesse, 'Wahlen, Wahlrecht, Wahlkampf und Wahlverhalten in der Bundesrepublik Deutschland', in *Neue Politische Literatur*, 31/1986, pp. 367–84.
2. See, most recently, Dolf Sternberger, *Grund und Abgrund der Macht. Über Legitimität von Regierungen*, new edn with 15 chs, Frankfurt/Main, 1986.
3. Cf. Guy Hermet, Richard Rose and Alain Rouquié (eds), *Elections without Choice*, London, 1978. The following work is from the Sternberger School: Hermann-Otto Leng, *Die allgemeine Wahl im bolschewistischen Staat. Theorie–Praxis–Genesis*, Meisenheim/Glan, 1973.

until now been inadequately researched if one considers the fact – often overlooked – that since the end of the Second World War only twenty-one countries have continuously remained democracies. Electoral researchers have often attempted to define the criteria for classifying an election as 'democratic'. There are no serious differences of opinion on this matter, although the opinions about what can be accurately described as 'a free election' often vary considerably. On the other hand, criticism of elections differs greatly, according to whether authoritarian, radical democratic or Marxist–Leninist positions are being represented, to name but three viewpoints. Incidentally, there have been no systematic studies analysing criticism of elections, and, typically, Marxist–Leninist science has been very reticent on this subject, indeed has never considered it.[4]

There is more material available in the case of historical electoral research, which must be based on aggregate figures. Here, the Norwegian social scientist Stein Rokkan, who is also highly regarded in West Germany, deserves special mention. In numerous studies, which are impressive both theoretically and empirically, he has introduced complex theories to explain the comparative development of mass democracies, and has repeatedly shown the connection between industrialisation and democratisation, noting how the characteristic lines of conflict ('cleavages') vary from country to country.[5] Amongst German-speaking social scientists, Otto Büsch has rendered particularly outstanding service to historical electoral research – not least in numerous anthologies of comparative studies.[6] Since the end of the 1970s, Jürgen W. Falter has provided more than a dozen methodical, very detailed studies of electoral successes of the National Socialists; the results of his research are shortly to be

4. For a GDR viewpoint see Herbert Graf and Günter Seiler, *Wahl und Wahlrecht im Klassenkampf*, Berlin (East), 1971.

5. Stein Rokkan, *Citizens, Elections, Parties: Approaches to the Comparative Study of the Processes of Development*, Oslo, 1970. See also Seymour M. Lipset and Stein Rokkan (eds), *Party Systems and Voter Alignments: Cross-National Perspectives*, New York, 1967.

6. See Otto Büsch, Monika Wölk and Wolfgang Wölk (eds), *Wählerbewegung in der deutschen Geschichte. Analysen und Berichte zu den Reichstagswahlen 1871–1933*, Berlin, 1978; Otto Büsch (ed.), *Wählerbewegung in der europäischen Geschichte*, Berlin, 1980; Otto Büsch and Peter Steinbach (eds), *Vergleichende europäische Wahlgeschichte. Eine Anthologie. Beiträge zur historischen Wahlforschung vornehmlich West- und Nordeuropas*, Berlin, 1983.

integrated into one large volume. Historical electoral research is important because it analyses and compares individual cases, instead of building abstract models.

There are currently a number of standard works giving an overview of the subject discussed in Chapter 3: elections and electoral systems in different countries. One of the most important is Dieter Nohlen's compendious work *Wahlsysteme der Welt*, initiated in research at Heidelberg University.[7] Unfortunately the mammoth project *Die Wahl der Parlamente*, which was also started at Heidelberg, is progressing rather slowly.[8] Four further modern anthologies providing an excellent overview of electoral systems in democracies are also to be recommended. Vernon Bogdanor and Arend Lijphart each edited or co-edited two of the four volumes. Bogdanor's two readers are divided according to countries, and Lijphart's according to problem areas.[9] Most of the contributions to these volumes are refreshingly undogmatic. Pleas for a specific voting-system, which once tended to predominate, are now giving way to a more strongly empirical approach – with the result that no particular voting-system is preferred. Samuel E. Finer's reader, with its programmatic title *Adversary Politics and Electoral Reform*,[10] still holds its place as a pioneering work on the subject of electoral reform. By 'adversary politics' Finer means politics which, owing to the conditions imposed by a relative-majority system, lead to continual changes of power and hence encourage a zig-zag policy – in other words, discontinuity. A recent anthology edited by Serge Noiret (1990) is particularly concerned with the current level of

7. Dieter Nohlen, *Wahlsysteme der Welt. Daten und Analysen. Ein Handbuch*, Munich, 1978. See also Dieter Nohlen, *Wahlrecht und Parteiensystem*, Opladen, 1986.

8. To date only the volumes on Europe and Africa have been published: *Die Wahl der Parlamente und anderer Staatsorgane. Ein Handbuch*, vol. 1: Dolf Sternberger and Bernhard Vogel (eds), *Europa* (published in two halves), Berlin, 1969; vol. 2: Franz Nuscheler and Klaus Ziemer (eds), *Politische Organisation und Repräsentation in Afrika* (published in two halves), Berlin, 1978.

9. Vernon Bogdanor and David Butler (eds), *Democracy and Elections: Electoral Systems and their Political Consequences*, Cambridge, 1983; Vernon Bogdanor (ed.), *Representatives of the People? Parliamentarians and Constituents in Western Democracies*, London, 1985; Arend Lijphart and Bernard Grofman (eds), *Choosing an Electoral System: Issues and Alternatives*, New York, 1984; Bernard Grofman and Arend Lijphart (eds), *Electoral Laws and their Political Consequences*, New York, 1986.

10. Samuel E. Finer, *Adversary Politics and Electoral Reform*, London, 1975.

research on electoral reform in selected European countries (Belgium, West Germany, France, the United Kingdom, Italy, Spain) and elucidates both differences and astonishing parallels.[11]

In view of the large number of comparative works, some of which have been inspired by the direct elections to the European Parliament and its attempts to standardise electoral law, Arend Lijphart (who has himself made important contributions in this area) may be accused of exaggerating when he writes that 'the study of electoral systems is undoubtedly the most underdeveloped subject in political science'.[12] However, there are undoubtedly gaps in the research. There is no counterpart for the German Kaiserreich to Eberhard Schanbacher's thorough study of the Weimar Republic,[13] which overestimates the significance of the proportional voting system for the downfall of the first German democracy.[14] Also, while there is a large amount of literature concerning the functioning of the British relative-majority system,[15] literature concerning the French absolute-majority system is nowhere near as extensive. The difference may be owing to the long tradition attached to the British method and its influence over other countries.[16]

The area of electoral sociology is also well served by the available literature. Back in 1965 Nils Diederich published a work comparing German, British and French electoral studies and highlighting individual characteristics.[17] If such a study were carried out now, it would probably arrive at the conclusion

11. Serge Noiret (ed.), *Stratégies politiques et électorales: aux origines des modes de scrutin en Europe aux XIXème et XXème siècles*, Baden-Baden, 1990.

12. Lijphart, in *Electoral Studies*, 4/1985, p. 3.

13. Eberhard Schanbacher, *Parlamentarische Wahlen und Wahlsystem in der Weimarer Republik. Wahlgesetzgebung und Wahlreform im Reich und in den Ländern*, Düsseldorf, 1982.

14. Cf. Hans Fenske, *Wahlrecht und Parteiensystem. Ein Beitrag zur deutschen Parteiengeschichte*, Frankfurt/Main, 1972, esp. pp. 106–45.

15. See for example David Butler's standard work, *The British Electoral System since 1918*, 2nd edn, Oxford, 1963; also David Butler, *Governing without a Majority: Dilemmas for Hung Parliaments in Britain*, London, 1983.

16. The following is without doubt still one of the most important studies: Peter Campbell, *French Electoral Systems and Elections since 1789*, 2nd edn, London, 1965.

17. Nils Diederich, *Empirische Walhforschung. Konzeptionen und Methoden im internationalen Vergleich*, Cologne and Opladen, 1965. The author also considers American electoral studies.

6

that the specific differences have become less significant. Whilst Diederich was forced to speak of the 'comparatively modest electoral literature available in West Germany',[18] the situation today is quite different. Indeed, with some German researchers one occasionally questions whether their theoretical and empirical ideals are matched by their efforts. As in the case of electoral systems, there are numerous comparative studies on the subject of voting-behaviour.[19]

The periodical *Electoral Studies* – with a prestigious international editorial advisory board – has been published since 1982, under the aegis of two men: the Briton David Butler, of Nuffield College, Oxford, who helped draw up the famous studies of British election campaigns since the Second World War,[20] and the Swede Bo Särlvik. This journal is devoted to the field of electoral sociology. It documents and analyses every election in a democracy with a population of over one million (plus Iceland, Luxembourg and Malta), thereby providing the reader with reliable information that might otherwise be difficult to obtain.[21]

The subject discussed in Chapter 4 of this study – elections and voting-rights in West Germany – is not only well-documented by official statistics (many countries would do well to follow West Germany's example, particularly in the compilation of representative electoral statistics) but also extensively researched. One could hardly call it a Cinderella subject, although admittedly not all areas are well covered and there are still some gaps. Erhard H. M. Lange examined the structure of voting-rights up until the Bundeswahlgesetz (Electoral Law) of 1975 and revealed the dominance of political pragmatism. Rüdiger Bredthauer proves the same to be true for the dispute regarding the electoral system during the Grand Coalition.[22] In

18. Ibid., p. 2.

19. Cf. Russell J. Dalton, Scott Flanagan and Paul Beck (eds), *Electoral Change in Advanced Industrial Democracies*, Princeton, NJ, 1984; Ivor Crewe and David Denver (eds), *Electoral Change in Western Democracies*, London and Sydney, 1985.

20. The most recent is David Butler and Dennis Kavanagh, *The British General Election of 1987*, London, 1988.

21. For information on earlier periods see Thomas T. Mackie and Richard Rose (eds), *The International Almanac of Electoral History*, 2nd edn, London, 1982.

22. See Erhard H. M. Lange, *Wahlrecht und Innenpolitik. Entstehungsgeschichte und Analyse der Wahlgesetzgebung und Wahlrechtsdiskussion im westlichen Nach-*

the first two decades of the Federal Republic, when there was considerable controversy in the political arena, among political scientists and in the media regarding the introduction of a majority electoral system, the academic camp which advocated a majority system was dominant, although individual supporters argued their cases in differing ways. The 'Cologne School', under their doyen Ferdinand A. Hermens, aimed to create and secure at almost any price a majority capable of governing by institutional means, and hence showed themselves extremely flexible with regard to the actual form which this majority electoral system should take.[23] By contrast, the 'Heidelberg School', led by Dolf Sternberger,[24] attached primary importance to the role of the voter and initially considered the majority system as primarily a 'vote for a personality'. The British relative-majority system with its one-man constituencies received strong support, not least because of its simplicity and because of the supposed connection between the voters and those elected.

Following the reform discussions at the time of the Grand Coalition, a number of noteworthy studies appeared. Hans Meyer combined his uncompromising preference for proportional representation with a reclassification of the electoral systems and strove to overcome the old conflict between proportional representation and the first-past-the-post system.[25] Whilst Hermens continues to view a majority system as a necessity,[26] Dolf Sternberger seems to have come to terms – 'in view of the long period of validity of the law'[27] – with the

---

kriegsdeutschland 1945–1956, Meisenheim/Glan, 1975; Rüdiger Bredthauer, *Das Wahlsystem als Objekt von Politik und Wissenschaft. Die Wahlsystemdiskussion in der BRD 1967/68 als politische und wissenschaftliche Auseinandersetzung*, Meisenheim/Glan, 1973.

23. See Ferdinand A. Hermens, *Demokratie oder Anarchie? Untersuchung über die Verhältniswahl* (1941), 2nd edn, Cologne and Opladen, 1968.

24. See Dolf Sternberger, *Die große Wahlreform. Zeugnisse einer Bemühung*, Cologne and Opladen, 1964.

25. Hans Meyer, *Wahlsystem und Verfassungsordnung. Bedeutung und Grenzen wahlsystematischer Gestaltung nach dem Grundgesetz*, Frankfurt/Main, 1973.

26. See Ferdinand A. Hermens, 'Evaluating Electoral Systems', in Max Kaase (ed.), *Politische Wissenschaft und politische Ordnung. Analysen zu Theorie und Empirie demokratischer Regierungsweise. Festschrift zum 65. Geburtstag von Rudolf Wildenmann*, Opladen, 1986, pp. 233–52.

27. Sternberger, *Grund und Abgrund der Macht*, p. 347.

proportional representation system. In the controversy over the relative merits of proportional representation and first-past-the-post systems – an academic theoretical dispute with no political consequences – the effective changes in voting-rights in West Germany (for example, introduction of the two-ballot system) have been overlooked, although they have by no means been devoid of consequences.[28]

The analysis of voting-behaviour in West Germany has long since outstripped research into electoral systems. Whilst the first Bundestag elections were analysed only sporadically,[29] the last few elections have received considerable attention. In addition to the publications of the Godesberg infas-Institut and the Mannheim 'Forschungsgruppe Wahlen', mention should be made of the regular analyses (since the Bundestag election of 1965) by Werner Kaltefleiter and by Max Kaase and Hans-Dieter Klingemann. Whilst Kaltefleiter's approach is methodical rather than pragmatic, the volumes published by Kaase and Klingemann attempt to combine empirical precision with ambitious theoretical analysis. Research into voting-behaviour in West Germany is by no means limited to analysis of Bundestag elections, but also includes analysis of regional elections and studies of, for example, non-voters and the influence of lifestyles on voting-behaviour. Several of these aspects have been explored by Wilhelm Bürklin, with particular emphasis on the theory of changes in values.[30] It is difficult to give an overview which comes even halfway to being properly representative. In this respect, a reliable statistical documentation such as the one by Ritter and Niehuss is extremely useful.[31]

28. See Eckhard Jesse, *Wahlrecht zwischen Kontinuität und Reform. Eine Analyse der Wahlsystemdiskussion und der Wahlrechtsänderungen in der Bundesrepublik Deutschland 1949–1983*, Düsseldorf, 1985, esp. pp. 211–367.

29. For 1949: Jürgen W. Falter, 'Kontinuität und Neubeginn. Die Bundestagswahl 1949 zwischen Weimar und Bonn', *Politische Vierteljahresschrift*, 22/1981, pp. 236–63. For 1953: Wolfgang Hirsch-Weber and Klaus Schütz, *Wähler und Gewählte. Eine Untersuchung der Bundestagswahlen 1953*, Berlin and Frankfurt/Main, 1957. For 1957: Erwin Faul (ed.), *Wahlen und Wähler in Westdeutschland*, Villingen, 1960. A bibliography for Bundestag elections up to 1983 can be found in Peter Schindler (ed.), *Datenhandbuch zur Geschichte des Deutschen Bundestags 1980 bis 1984. Fortschreibungs- und Ergänzungsband zum Datenhandbuch Bundestag 1949 bis 1982*, Baden-Baden, 1984, pp. 128–32.

30. See Wilhelm Bürklin, *Wählerverhalten und Wertewandel*, Opladen, 1988.

31. Gerhard A. Ritter and Merith Niehuss, *Wahlen in der Bundesrepublik Deutschland. Bundestags- und Landtagswahlen 1946–1987*, Munich, 1987.

As this brief survey of the state of research shows, the number of relevant works is legion. A definite weakness of many books is that they discuss electoral systems, empirical research into elections, and the theoretical aspects of democracy in isolation from each other. This book seeks to remedy the situation by embracing all three levels of inquiry.

2
Elections and Democracy

Definitions

In a technical sense, elections are 'a way of forming corporations or of appointing a person into an office'.[1] This definition, however, only considers the method of appointment. In this sense, elections differ from other methods of appointing authority primarily used in the past. Apart from seizing power by violent means (for example, in a putsch), alternative methods are drawing lots or blood succession. As drawing lots is based on chance and is consequently beyond the principle of rationality, it is hardly used any more. One tends to fall back on this method only in exceptional cases (for instance, in the event of a tie). No democracy could justify the practice of blood succession. Today, a certain role is also played by co-opting (i.e. a political corporation supplementing itself) and *ex officio* appointment ('automatic' acceptance into a corporation on the grounds of high office). Electoral sociology views voting as a form of political behaviour which takes place (a) on a huge scale, (b) at regular intervals under comparative conditions, and (c) via a method which is easy to ascertain in quantitative terms.[2] Hence, if one wishes to observe this form of political participation, the conditions under which it occurs are ideal.

Today almost all states conduct elections: for example, in the 1970s, of the 136 current member states of the United Nations only eight had not held any elections in the preceding ten years.[3] The differences, nevertheless, are obvious. Dieter Nohlen,[4] like many others, differentiates between *competitive*,

1. Dieter Nohlen, *Wahlsysteme der Welt. Daten und Analysen. Ein Handbuch*, Munich, 1978, p. 18.
2. Werner Kaltefleiter and Peter Nißen, *Empirische Wahlforschung. Eine Einführung in Theorie und Technik*, Paderborn, 1980, p. 15.
3. See Guy Hermet, Richard Rose and Alan Rouquié (eds), Preface to *Elections without Choice*, London, 1978, p. vii.
4. Nohlen, *Wahlsysteme der Welt*, esp. pp. 18–22.

Table 2.1 The significance and function of elections

	Competitive elections	Semi-competitive elections	Non-competitive elections
Significance for the political process	High	Low	Very low
Opportunities for choice	High	Limited	None
Freedom of election	Guaranteed	Limited	Abolished
Power is questioned	Yes	No	No
Legitimises the political system	Yes	Sometimes attempted	Never/rarely attempted
Type of political system	Democratic	Authoritarian	Totalitarian

Source: Dieter Nohlen, *Wahlrecht und Parteiensystem*, Opladen, 1986, p. 21.

non-competitive and *semi-competitive elections*. A *competitive* election is one where the voter can exert real influence on the result of the election. This occurs in democratic constitutional states. *Non-competitive* elections are those where the people do not have any opportunity to express their opinions by means of the election. This was formerly the case, for example, in elections in communist countries. *Semi-competitive* elections – as the expression suggests – do not fit into either of the above categories. This type is characteristic of many developing countries.

This classification of elections corresponds, to a large extent, to the conventional distinction between democratic, totalitarian and authoritarian states, even though the distinction between non-competitive and semi-competitive is just as difficult to make as that between totalitarian and authoritarian, and there does not appear to be any agreement on this matter, as most authoritarian states are founded on non-competitive elections.[5] In Af-

5. For a summary of this see Dieter Nohlen, 'Die politischen Systeme der Dritten Welt', in Klaus von Beyme, Ernst-Otto Czempiel, Peter Graf Kielmansegg and Peter Schmoock (eds), *Politikwissenschaft. Eine Grundlegung*, vol. 1: *Theorien und Systeme*, Stuttgart, 1987, pp. 200–47.

rica, for example, democratic elections are by no means part of everyday political life. South Africa is not the only country whose government lacks legitimacy.[6]

The significance, function and legitimising principle of an election vary according to which form of election one is considering (see Table 2.1). In Western democracies in particular, elections serve the functions of legitimacy, participation and control,[7] whilst those in other systems tend rather to serve the purposes of identification, integration and acclaim. In this, the functions may naturally overlap, because even in democracies elections make an important contribution towards integrating the citizens, just as in dictatorships they may likewise serve to legitimise those elected.

Elections must be understood in their entirety. The actual act of voting is preceded by the presentation of candidates and followed by the counting and weighing of the votes.[8] The criteria of 'freedom of election' (see below, pp. 21–4) must apply to all three areas. A democratic election loses its meaning if the presentation of candidates deprives the electorate of any power before the election even takes place – for example, by means of 'single candidates'. If voting is structured so that it qualifies or revises the electorate's decision at a later stage – for instance, by preferential treatment of certain groups – the election would likewise become nonsensical.

History

Until well into the eighteenth century (and in some cases into the nineteenth), elections had virtually no significance. Class-bound bodies consisting of the nobility, the clergy and the town councils were not elected. If the principle of the election existed at all, it only applied within a certain social class. The revol-

6. See for example Günter Krabbe, 'Wahlen gelten als unafrikanisch. Demokratische Systeme haben es vorerst schwer, gegen die Tradition anzukommen', *Frankfurter Allgemeine Zeitung*, 13 November 1985, p. 12.

7. For a modification see Rainer-Olaf Schultze, 'Wahlen und politischer Wandel. Überlegungen zur historisch-politischen Kontextdetermination von Wahlfunktion und Wählerverhalten', *Politische Bildung*, 19.2/1986, pp. 18–32.

8. Heribert Westerath, *Die Wahlverfahren und ihre Vereinbarkeit mit den demokratischen Anforderungen an das Wahlrecht*, Berlin, 1955, p. 68.

utions in France and America, which caused far-reaching changes, and which in many people's opinions took up and further developed the inheritance of antiquity, brought into force the principle of people's sovereignty. The basis of legitimacy for political power began to change. Hence democratic elections have only been accepted gradually and after intense disputes. This process took place in various phases.[9] In the nineteenth century the ambitious bourgeoisie demanded political influence and sought to free itself from the monarchy's tutelage.

For the working class, the struggle for universal suffrage was an important and integral part of their main demands. The spread of democratic elections, which was both encouraged and hindered by various different factors, did not proceed uniformly in European countries. The German Kaiserreich was one of the first states whose national parliament, the Reichstag, was democratically elected. Admittedly, the electorate could not determine the executive, and, because the emperor still held the balance of power, it remained largely excluded from any effective influence, even though the Reichstag was responsible for legislation and for the budget. In the United Kingdom, on the other hand, the 'parliamentarisation' of the executive took place much more quickly and as part of an almost continual process, although citizens were only granted the vote in stages by the individual electoral law reforms of 1832, 1867, 1884, 1918 and 1928. Gabriel Almond, one of the doyens of research into political culture, rightly places his main emphasis on the strategy of political elites:

> Threats to a regime resulting from dissatisfaction . . . can sometimes be directly overcome, as was the case in Great Britain's democratisation process in the nineteenth century. In the course of this debate it was a question not of the 'either/or' of universal suffrage, but of a gradual, limited expansion of the right to vote as a reaction to those sections of the population which were most strongly mobilised. Bismarck's strategy in Germany avoided widespread demands by the

9. Cf. various essays in Seymour M. Lipset and Stein Rokkan (eds), *Party Systems and Voter Alignments: Cross-National Perspectives*, New York, 1967. See also Jürgen Kohl, 'Zur langfristigen Entwicklung der politischen Partizipation in Westeuropa', in Peter Steinbach (ed.), *Probleme politischer Partizipation im Modernisierungsprozeß*, Stuttgart, 1982, pp. 473–503.

middle and working classes for unlimited voting rights by making tactical, shrewd concessions: welfare-state concesssions to please the workers, trading-concessions to please the industrialists and major landowners, and an aggressive foreign policy which appealed to everyone. Bismarck's strategy of using a distributive policy as a means of moderating and restricting demands for greater participation is likewise used today in a number of Third World countries, particularly in South Korea and Taiwan.[10]

Admittedly Almond is wrong regarding universal suffrage during Bismarck's time, for it was in fact this which was used to ward off more far-reaching demands (for instance, for the parliamentarisation of the Reich government), but his argument makes the strategy of political elites plausible.

In making an evaluation, then, parliamentarisation must be seen in conjunction with the introduction of universal suffrage. Both factors must be equally fulfilled before one can talk of a democratic system. As shown in Table 2.2, the two developments have not occurred simultaneously. In some countries universal suffrage (for men) only occurred after parliamentarisation, whilst in others the reverse was true. Stein Rokkan

> classifies European countries between two extremes: the English model of a slow, gradual expansion of voting rights with no reversals but with long periods of formal recognition of inequalities, and the French model of an early and sudden introduction of universal and equal civil rights, but with frequent reversals and the tendency to exploit the support of the masses by means of plebiscites.[11]

Germany, with its radical changes, clearly belongs to the 'French category'. However, there are many points in favour of the 'English model', which entailed fewer 'costs'. However, one must also guard against presenting certain models as absolute.

The introduction of universal suffrage frequently occurred at the same time as the introduction of proportional representation. It is noticeable 'that in the course of approximately 100 years a process of change has taken place which resulted in an

10. Gabriel A. Almond, 'Politische Kultur-Forschung – Rückblick und Ausblick', in Dirk Berg-Schlosser and Jakob Schissler (eds), *Politische Kultur in Deutschland. Bilanz und Perspektiven der Forschung*, Opladen, 1987, p. 38.
11. Kohl, in Steinbach, *Probleme politischer Partizipation*, p. 487.

Table 2.2 Parliamentarisation and democratisation of the vote in
Western European countries

Country	Year of parliamentarisation	Percentage of people eligible to vote[a]	Introduction of universal suffrage (for men)
Belgium	1831	1.1	1894/1919
United Kingdom	1832–5	3.3	1918
Switzerland	1848	22.0	1848
Italy	1861	1.9	1913/1919
Netherlands	1868	2.8	1918
Luxembourg	1868	2.9	1919
France	(1814–30)	(0.3)	
	1875	27.0	1848
Norway	1884	5.2	1900
Denmark	1901	16.4	1849
Iceland	1903	9.8	1916
Sweden	1917	19.4	1911
Finland	1917	43.0	1907
Germany	1919	59.4	1871
Austria	1919	55.4	1907
Ireland	1922	47.3	1918

(a) In the year of parliamentarisation (percentage of the population).
Source: Jürgen Kohl, 'Zur langfristigen Entwicklung der politischen Partizipation in West Europa', in Peter Steinbach (ed.), *Probleme politischer Partizipation im Modernisierungsprozeß*, Stuttgart, 1982, p. 488.

expansion of active citizenship from an average of less than 10% to over 80% of the adult population and hence led to new classes and social strata of the population being incorporated into the political system on a huge scale'.[12] This process, which occurred at different speeds in different countries, took place roughly between the middle of the nineteenth century and the middle of the twentieth century.

Identity Theory versus Competitive Theory

'The academic theory of elections received its final, indeed decisive, impetus from Josef Schumpeter in 1942.'[13] This may

12. Ibid., p. 481.
13. Philipp, Herder-Dorneich, 'Wahl und Wahlmechanismus', in Franz Geiß, Philipp Herder-Dorneich and Wilhelm Weber (eds), *Der Mensch im sozio-ökonomischen Prozeß*, Berlin, 1969, p. 61.

sound like an exaggeration – after all, a large number of political theoreticians had dealt with the theory of elections much earlier than this – but it is true in principle because Schumpeter, in Herder-Dorneich's words, virtually completed a 'Copernican change in electoral theory'.[14] He did this by no longer assuming that the nation had 'a fixed and rational opinion about every individual issue' and by rejecting the idea that one of the tasks of democracy was to permit people to vote for 'representatives' 'who ensure that this opinion is put into practice'.[15] In this concept of democracy, which Schumpeter misleadingly characterised as the 'classical theory', the established 'voters' will' predominated, whilst the election of representatives was merely a technical means to an end – the implementation of the people's will. Schumpeter, on the other hand, reversed the relationship between and significance of these two factors.

'The democratic method is the institutional order for the achievement of political decisions in which individuals obtain the authority to make decisions by means of a competitive battle for the votes of the people.'[16] This is Schumpeter's famous definition of the competitive theory. This stands in fundamental opposition to the identity theory of democracy, of which Jean-Jacques Rousseau is considered the 'classic' advocate. Schumpeter summarises this theory as follows: 'The democratic method is the institutional order for the achievement of political decisions which realises the common weal by allowing the nation to make up its own mind about controversial issues, by electing people who have to meet in order to implement the nation's will.'[17]

In these rival models of democracy, elections have differing functions. The following discussion is less concerned with an authentic reproduction of Schumpeter's and Rousseau's theories than with highlighting the two fundamentally opposing positions. The comparison must take place on the same level: either inherent criticism of the theory, or else criticism of the practice which is legitimised by certain theories. If, when considering

14. Ibid.
15. Joseph A. Schumpeter, *Kapitalismus, Sozialismus und Demokratie* (1942), 3rd edn, Munich, 1972, p. 427.
16. Ibid., p. 428.
17. Ibid., p. 397.

the identity theory, one primarily concentrates on the dangers inherent in it and hence considers mainly the *reality* of those systems which adopt the identity theory, but explains the competitive theory more in terms of its *theoretical framework*, one is being inconsistent and is measuring with two different yardsticks.

The identity theory of democracy, otherwise known simply as the *identity theory* (or *identity democracy*), is based, as the name suggests, on an identity between the rulers and the ruled. Rousseau's theory negates the principle of representation. It is not possible, he claims, to represent the common weal, and every law would require confirmation by the people: 'The idea of representation belongs to more modern times. . . . In the old republics, indeed even in monarchies, the people never had representatives.'[18] Accordingly, in the identity theory, representation can only be justified by the size of the state – as a type of 'technical aid'. In consequence, the decisions of the representatives must always be linked to the wishes of the people. The model of Soviet democracy advocated by parts of the 'New Left' towards the end of the 1960s is also based on this theoretical assumption. According to the identity theory, elections only serve to translate the 'people's will' into reality. This will, however, is considered by advocates of the identity theory to be homogeneous. Rousseau even goes as far as to say that the common will (*volonté générale*), which is aimed at the common good and is 'always right',[19] must not allow itself to be confused with the sum total of the people's individual wills (*volonté de tous*). Therefore a legislature (*législateur*) is needed whose 'higher insight . . . raises itself above the field of vision of the individual person'.[20] Consequently, this concept leaves no legitimate place for elections in the sense of selection.

For many pluralist theoreticians, Rousseau is not the progenitor of democracy, but the progenitor of 'totalitarian democracy' (Jacor L. Talmon). In view of the parallels to dictatorships, for example, Gerhard A. Ritter says of the divinely inspired 'legislature', a type of *deus ex machina*: 'This concept in many respects anticipates the role of the "Führer", which later became reality,

18. Cf. Jean-Jacques Rousseau, *Du contrat social* (1762), bk 4, ch. 4.
19. Ibid., bk 2, ch. 3.
20. Ibid., bk 2, ch. 7.

or rather of the vanguard of the proletariat.'[21] Theoreticians of the left and the right are similar both in their justifications of power in totalitarian states and in their basic theoretical concepts. For example, Carl Schmitt and Johannes Agnoli interpret democracy as 'identity between the rulers and the ruled'.[22] According to whether more emphasis is placed on unity between rulers and ruled or on the 'uniformity' of the people's will, one can talk of either the identity theory or the homogeneity theory.

The 'true' exponent of the competitive theory of democracy, otherwise known as the *competitive theory* (or *competitive democracy*) is considered to be Joseph A. Schumpeter, although it naturally also has important roots in the thinking of the eighteenth and nineteenth centuries.[23] Unlike the identity theory, this theory considers it imperative that the nation elect a government. The elected representatives, who are not bound to take instructions from the electors during their time in office, surrender themselves to the vote of the electorate once the legislative period is over. Hence, in this concept, democracy does not mean rule over the people but rule with the consent of the people. In this sense, the competitive theory is oriented towards the idea of representation. The act of voting to 'enthrone' the representatives is considered decisively important. In the competitive theory, there is no 'clear and definite common weal which the entire nation would agree on or could be made to agree on by the use of rational arguments'.[24] Political decision-making and the implementation of those decisions, it is argued, should take place by means of an open process of dispute between the heterogeneous group interests. The consequence of

21. Gerhard A. Ritter, '"Direkte Demokratie" und Rätewesen in Geschichte und Theorie', in Erwin K. Scheuch (ed.), *Die Wiedertäufer der Wohlstandsgesellschaft*, 2nd edn, Cologne, 1968, p. 217. For an alternative opinion, see for example Iring Fetscher, *Rousseaus politische Philosophie* (1962), 2nd edn, Neuwied and Berlin, 1968.
22. See Carl Schmitt, *Die geistesgeschichtliche Lage des heutigen Parlamentarismus* (1923/6), 4th edn, Berlin, 1969, p. 20; Johannes Agnoli, *Die Transformation der Demokratie*, Frankfurt/Main, p. 70.
23. This is not strictly true, inasmuch as the identity theory generally sees itself as the 'classical' theory of democracy. The competitive theory, however, likewise has its 'classical' roots. Cf. Hans Kremendahl, *Pluralismustheorie in Deutschland*, Leverkusen, 1977, p. 41.
24. Schumpeter, *Kapitalismus, Sozialismus und Demokratie*, p. 399.

19

this is that the election confers responsibility on the people to select a person who will be responsible for arranging public affairs.

Schumpeter understood his theory predominantly as a *method*. Regardless of whether there is any truth in the popular belief that his is a 'formalistic perception of democracy' and a 'so-called "value-free" image of democracy',[25] pluralist theoreticians have enlarged upon his theory and added normative elements. Hence the acceptance of a democratic minimum consensus is just as much an integral part of the pluralist theory (at least in the German version) as the emphasis on participatory aspects. Ernst Fraenkel claims that this has the following consequences regarding elections:

> The competitive theory of democracy does not do justice to the requirements it should face if it does not consider parliamentary elections to be anything more than a personal plebiscite between two personalities who are scrambling to reach the office of head of government.[26]

The choice between individuals needs to be supplemented by a choice of ideas and aims.

The identity theory is based on the idea that the concept of representation is to be rejected and that the people's will is homogeneous and objectively recognisable. In terms of elections, this means at best an acceptance of proportional representation, in which the 'people's will' is faithfully reflected in parliament – if indeed an election with alternatives is considered necessary at all, in view of the fact that the people's will is deemed to be established.

The competitive theory, on the other hand, rejects the principles of identity and homogeneity and by contrast declares its support for the opinion that democracy requires political leadership. The creation of a government is in fact seen as one of the main functions of elections.[27] The consequence of this in terms of the electoral process is that, in principle, the first-past-the-

---

25. Kremendahl, *Pluralismustheorie in Deutschland*, pp. 41–2.

26. Ernst Fraenkel, *Deutschland und die westlichen Demokratien* (1964), 7th edn, Stuttgart, 1979, p. 65.

27. See Schumpeter, *Kapitalismus, Sozialismus und Demokratie*, p. 432.

post system is preferred. Hence it is hardly surprising that Schumpeter explicitly rejects proportional representation.[28] However, whether support for the competitive theory of democracy must *necessarily* be combined with a plea for the first-past-the-post system is a different matter. This is surely more a question of a country's specific constellation (the party structure, political culture, historical development, and so on), as well as of the individual value premises of the observer. Whilst it is certainly possible for the competitive theory to be combined with proportional representation, it is not possible to combine the identity theory and the majority system (in view of the strict orientation towards the 'people's will'). No supporters of the identity theory also support a majority electoral system.

Only the competitive theory of democracy (in connection with the pluralist theory[29]) fulfils the demands for democratic legitimacy of a political form of order. The election takes the people's sovereignty into account; however, the elected government is by no means obliged to adhere to the 'people's will' in every dispute, and hence the people's sovereignty is not made absolute. In the identity theory, on the other hand, democratic legitimacy is already present when the state claims to translate the (true) people's will into reality – regardless of whether this is really based on the empirically ascertainable will of the population, and also regardless of to what extent it affects certain basic and human rights.

'Freedom of Election'

'Freedom of election', which forms a central part of the democratic concept of elections,[30] must be understood in a broad sense. Ernst Fraenkel correctly asserts:

> Freedom of election may only serve as a suitable criterion to explain the different characters of the democratic regime of the FRG and the

28. See ibid.
29. This addition is necessary because Schumpeter's concept of the competitive theory does not adequately protect natural rights, such as human dignity.
30. Cf. Bernhard Vogel, Dieter Nohlen and Rainer-Olaf Schultze, *Wahlen in Deutschland. Theorie–Geschichte–Dokumente 1848–1970*, Berlin, 1970, esp. pp. 2–6.

pseudo-democratic regime of the GDR if the individual electoral process is understood, not as an isolated process, but as part of a continual process. Freedom of election means more than the election taking place according to the rules; it means agreeing with the values which are inseparably connected with the expression 'freedom'. Hence it is not enough to restrict oneself to the analysis of the more technical legal conditions of electoral laws.[31]

In this sense 'freedom of election' should include the following criteria, without making them absolute: freedom of choice (choice of several different options); freedom of options (competition); and the freedom to revise one's vote (decisions apply to a fixed term).

(a) Freedom of choice   The citizen has to make his decision between several (at least two) election proposals. An election always implies choice. In order that the voter should possess an adequate information base for his vote, the freedom of press and information must be guaranteed. Furthermore, the freedom to found parties is just as much a *conditio sine qua non* as the parties' having equal opportunities (in principle) for competition. Incidentally, groups whose aim is to abolish democratic elections once they have attained power may be banned. If, in this way, freedom of choice is limited under some circumstances (*party* elements), it is in any case limited by the nomination of candidates, in which most voters do not participate (*individual* elements).

(b) Freedom of options   The freedom to choose loses its meaning if the available options do not offer any real alternatives. A 'party system' which is controlled by a single party does not deserve this name. Competition is literally essential for 'freedom of options', but this does not necessarily mean that the parties must have opposing positions on all possible problems. Admittedly, the alternatives should not merely be limited to a choice between different individuals, as is suggested by Schumpeter's

---

31. Ernst Fraenkel, 'Strukturanalyse der modernen Demokratie', in *Aus Politik und Zeitgeschichte*, supplement to *Das Parlament*, B49/1969, p. 4.

view that 'voters do not have any decision-making powers in disputes'.[32]

The competitive theory of democracy, in its true sense, means that elections do not only determine the future head of government but also decide on alternative solutions, and issue a verdict about the policy which the majority party represents and at the same time a verdict about the policy which the minority party has advocated.[33]

(c) The freedom to revise one's vote   Freedom of choice and freedom of options often become invalid if the election is not a decision which is limited to a fixed term. The electorate's influence can only be ensured and the opportunity of the rulers to misuse their power limited if the people's representatives subject themselves to the judgement of the voters at regular, predetermined and fairly close intervals. Therefore, election for life cannot be reconciled with the basic principles of a democratic order, where legitimacy derives from 'the mandate to rule for a fixed period' (Theodor Heuss). The voter must receive the opportunity to revise his vote: 'Any misuse of the entrusted office in the sense of establishing oneself permanently consequently leads to a loss of legitimacy.'[34] The loser in an election has to recognise his defeat and accept the (limited) rule of his victor. A person who stands for election with the aim of abolishing the electoral system is pushing the concepts of democracy to the point of absurdity.

If 'freedom of election' as characterised here does not exist or exists only in a very limited form, the election is stripped of its value. These criteria must be satisfied for an election to confer legitimacy and be properly democratic. If they are not satisfied, an electoral process which is in other respects perfect remains a farce. The evaluation of a political system depends fundamen-

32. Schumpeter, *Kapitalismus, Sozialismus und Demokratie*, p. 449. See likewise Wilhelm Hennis, 'Amtsgedanke und Demokratiebegriff' (1962), in Schumpeter, *Die mißverstandene Demokratie. Demokratie–Verfassung–Parlament. Studien zu deutschen Problemen*, Freiburg/Breisgau, 1973, p. 23ff.; Dolf Sternberger, *Grund und Abgrund der Macht. Über Legitimität von Regierungen*, new edn with 15 chs, Frankfurt/Main, 1986, pp. 231–3.

33. Fraenkel, *Deutschland und die westlichen Demokratien*, p. 65.

34. Dolf Sternberger, 'Herrschaft und Vereinbarung', *'Ich wünschte ein Bürger zu sein!'*, Frankfurt/Main, 1967, p. 67.

tally on the functions of its elections: if they fulfil a legitimising, participatory and controlling function and hence in certain circumstances contribute to a change of government, they are an *efficient part* of the constitution; if their function is largely decorative, they merely represent a *dignified part*[35] of the constitution.

Voting-Principles

Voting-principles have been developed (and have also changed) in the course of a process lasting centuries. Nowadays, these principles comprise the universal, direct, equal and secret vote. These principles apply to every election – regardless of what type of electoral process the legislator decides to employ.

The right to vote is *universal* when all citizens are entitled to it. The legislator does not have the right to dispute the rights of a section of citizens to vote – for whatever reason. Certain practical requirements must be fulfilled, though – for example, full citizenship, minimum age, nationality. In the past, the right to vote was often dependent on property ownership, education, tax payments, sex or religion.

The right to vote is *direct* when those eligible to vote vote for their representatives directly. The results of the election (and the distribution of seats) should depend solely on the citizens' votes. When voting commences, the influence of the party over the selection of candidates ends. Therefore it contravenes the basic principle of directness if a party changes the order of the list after the election. If an intermediate authority is elected which then appoints the representatives, the vote then becomes indirect. This would be unconstitutional. At all costs, one must refrain from making up the electorate's minds for them.

A vote is *equal* when every elector is granted the same number of votes. In addition, one vote cannot be worth more than another. This principle is intended to guarantee the equal influence of all voters on the result. Whilst in proportional representation 'equal', at least according to 'prevailing theory' in West Germany, means that the proportion of votes is equal to the

35. For an explanation of terms see Walter Bagehot's classical study *The English Constitution*, 1867.

proportion of success, in majority systems 'equality' refers to equality in the number of votes. A plural vote which, for example, would grant extra votes to parents of children not yet old enough to vote is lacking in legitimacy because it contravenes the principle of equality.

An election is *secret* when it is impossible for an individual to discover the electoral decision of another citizen. The voter must be certain that he is able to vote without any possible sanctions. The voter's open commitment to a party – for example in pressure groups – naturally remains unaffected by this. The basic principle of a secret election also applies to the preparations for elections, but at the same time, however, is limited to a certain extent: election proposals for parties who are not represented in parliament require a certain number of signatures in order to guarantee the seriousness of the candidate. It is not by chance that various advocates of the identity theory, such as Rousseau, Carl Schmitt and Marxist–Leninists, have reservations about the secret election.

The requirement that an election should be 'free', which is established in the constitutions of only a few countries, is not a classic election principle. It does not say anything about the technical structure of a system – the other voting-principles are adequate for this,[36] unless by 'free' one means elections which do not contain any obligation to vote. But, in view of the existing connotations of the word 'free', this could cause misunderstandings. If by 'free' one means 'freedom of choice', that is the same as to say that an election should be truly democratic. If it is interpreted to mean that the voter should not be placed under any compulsion, then ultimately it has the same meaning as 'secret', as defined above. Whether one decides on the broad or the narrow interpretation, to state, as a principle, that an election should be 'free' is merely question-begging, and does nothing to define what 'freedom of election' entails.

Criticism of Elections

Criticisms levelled at elections are very varied in nature. They range from objections which are also useful for reforms with

---

36. See also Nohlen, *Wahlsysteme der Welt*, p. 46.

reference to the structure of elections, to objections of principle which, rather than criticising the practice of elections, criticise democratic elections themselves. Whilst the following three forms of criticism are very different, they do have one thing in common: their orientation towards the identity theory of elections.

Conservative–Authoritarian Criticism

Today, conservative–authoritarian criticism no longer plays a very significant role in West Germany. Concepts of a corporate state are not popular. The principal and fundamental criticism which Winfried Martini levelled at elections[37] in his 1954 work *Das Ende aller Sicherheit*, which at the time was considered spectacular with its frequent reference to Carl Schmitt, today meets with hardly any response, even in (neo-)conservative circles. According to this theory, an election in which everyone can exercise the same influence must necessarily lead to problematic consequences, and equality does not do justice to the complicated demands made of the state: the voter, Martini argues, allows himself to be led by moods and emotions, is not concerned with politics, is clueless, ignorant, bewildered and irresponsible. The dependence on the oscillating will of the people endangers a policy aimed at continuity and long-term planning. Hence Martini wanted either to reduce universal suffrage to those decisions 'which still fall within the sphere of observation and interest of the voters and where they are there-fore capable of giving a rational judgement and where incorrect decisions only have limited effect', or to permit voting at all levels, but with no real consequences for 'major politics'.[38] He argued that, because of the 'universal *anonymity* of responsi-bility' ensured by the secret vote, political indifference was

37. Winfried Martini, *Das Ende aller Sicherheit*, Stuttgart, 1954. Theodor Es-chenburg evaluated Martini's work surprisingly 'gently'. See Theodor Eschen-burg, '*Das Ende aller Sicherheit*', *Der Wähler*, 5/1955, pp. 18–22. He agrees with Martini's analysis to a certain extent, but accuses him of being unable to suggest any democratic alternative to the parliamentary system of government. For an opposing view see Dolf Sternberger, 'Das Kind mit dem Bade ausgeschüttet', *Kriterien*, Frankfurt/Main, 1965, pp. 334–45. It is not surprising that Sternberger criticises Martini severely but does not make excessive demands on the voter. Admittedly, one could ask whether his fixation with elections as an act of trust perhaps in fact underestimates them.

38. Martini, *Das Ende aller Sicherheit*, p. 315.

growing. Nor did Martini shy away from improbable examples: 'The farmer, for example, who in former times had a picture of the Kaiser in his best room, had thereby made an *existential* political decision, and, the less it had been reflected upon, the more solid and justified it was.'[39] Martini's vague solution was an authoritarian state like Salazar's Portugal as it existed until the mid-1970s.

This position can be criticised for the way in which it simply equates modern democracy with the sovereignty of the people. 'Just like any other form of state, democracy does not say anything about the content of the will of the state, but only determines the mechanical conditions under which it should be formed. It is only a formal principle of organisation.'[40] Moreover, it is a misunderstanding to say that the representative democracy's ability to function – whereby principles such as the protection of minorities are fixed by the constitution – is based on the omniscience of the citizens, their knowledge of the facts, and their maturity. Survey results, according to Martini, showed that many decisions expect far too much of the voter and that he tends to react emotionally. In fact, the critic is wrong to attempt to ridicule the constitutional state with this argument, for representative democracy is not bound to an imperative mandate, however that may be interpreted. The objection that the majority of the population is not at all capable of appreciating the complexity of the problems awaiting decisions would only be conclusive in a plebiscitary democracy.

To discuss this position in detail would be rather like disturbing a corpse, because such ideas no longer play an important role in serious academic literature. Moreover, most of the theorists whom critics cite as an example of the continuing virulence of right-wing anti-democratic positions have fallen silent.

Marxist–Leninist Criticism

Marxist–Leninist criticism is based on the assumption that elections in 'bourgeois democracies' disguise their 'class character', whilst elections in 'socialist democracies' demonstrate the

39. Martini, *Freiheit auf Abruf. Die Lebenserwartung der Bundesrepublik*, Cologne and Berlin, 1960, p. 341.
40. Martini, *Das Ende aller Sicherheit*, p. 30.

power of the working class and legitimise it. Hence, in accordance with the identity theory, in a Marxist–Leninist state oppositional trends are an alien element. 'There neither existed nor do there exist social conditions and tasks or political forces and groups against which an opposition would have to direct itself.' They continue with disarming frankness:

> Demands for opposition lists and opposition parties in socialist countries are . . . the weapons of the opponents of socialism, the enemies of peace and of democracy. As the slogan of the imperialist plurality theory . . . they contradict the unity between people and state and their common interests.[41]

Although, in this context, elections may not under any circumstances question the rule of the 'working class', they nevertheless exist, because even Marxism–Leninists cannot escape the legitimising-power of elections. In claiming to know the course of history, they assume that the identity of people and state is fixed. In fact, such historicism is incompatible with democratic elections. It is self-evident that this position, which is based on an *a priori* common weal and, as such, views deviating opinions as heretical, cannot confer any legitimacy on an opinion oriented towards the principle of pluralism.

'Radical Democratic' Criticism

Radical democratic criticism, as exemplified by the criticism mounted by the 'New Left' towards the end of the 1960s or by the Greens since the beginning of the 1980s, deserves more intensive critical analysis. It assumes that elections in late-capitalist systems have declined enormously in significance or have even become completely insignificant. If this is true, then discussions about the electoral system and how it should be changed are of no importance.

> Elections in Western democracies are characterised today . . . by a loss of meaning as regards content, their function being predominantly to integrate and manipulate, and by the atomisation of the

41. Herbert Graf and Günter Seiler, *Wahl und Wahlrecht in Klassenkampf*, Berlin (East), 1971, pp. 207–8.

individual in the act of voting; but despite this loss of significance they are also characterised by propagandistic exaggeration of the significance of elections.[42]

Whilst the statist–authoritarian argument attacked elections mainly because of their dangerous consequences for the state, here the situation is literally reversed. Elections have become nothing more than a ritual. As early as 1962 Ekkehart Krippendorff was predicting the end of parliamentary opposition, hence implicitly casting doubt on the point of elections.[43] This position deserves more detailed recognition and critical analysis.

Krippendorff argued that election results in various countries had shown that governments could no longer be replaced by elections. From this he went on to discuss future developments, analysing in particular the function of parliamentary opposition. His intention was to develop an adequate alternative to party democracy. Parties used to represent certain social interests. Today, however, they see themselves principally as organisations which can secure election by *all* citizens. Purely by definition, there cannot be two 'people's parties' within the same state. The notion that there will always be conflict, that the concept of a just order will always be disputed, and that the government makes mistakes and can be changed by means of elections is one of the 'dogmas of liberal philosophy',[44] in Krippendorff's words. In fact, he claims, governments today possess an apparatus which allows them to avoid serious (economic) crises. Social science has learnt so much about researching and influencing opinion that is no longer possible to replace a governing party by means of an election. Hence only two possibilities remain open to the opposition: if they recognise the system as acceptable in principle, they have lost their justification for existence; if this is not the case, they must organise the victims' interests against the political system.

A parliamentary system based on an election between competing parties is only 'provisional', Krippendorff claims. The

42. Joachim Raschke, 'Mehrheitswahl – Mittel zur Demokratisierung oder Formierung der Gesellschaft?', in Winfried Steffani (ed.), *Parlamentarismus ohne Transparenz*, Opladen, 1971, p. 194.
43. Ekkehart Krippendorff, 'Das Ende des Parteienstaates?', *Der Monat*, 14.160/1962, pp. 64–70.
44. Ibid., p. 67.

less the opposition questions the entire system in principle, the sooner the party state will come to an end. The 'one-party state' which would then arise would not necessarily be an undesirable entity. Effective democracy within the party requires more commitment 'than exists today, at least in Western European democracies, in which the single act of voting pleasantly disguises the fact that the people are otherwise almost totally inactive'.[45]

Certainly, not all Krippendorff's concepts contradict the competitive theory of democracy. This is true, for example, of his theory that the government often has competitive advantages over the parliamentary opposition: the ability of the welfare state to reduce social tensions; the advantage of holding office and being able to 'time' measures and use state activities to influence opinion in favour of the government; traditional misunderstandings regarding the role of parliamentary opposition.

For these and other reasons, from the mid-1950s until approximately the mid-1970s 'opposition pessimism'[46] was rife, and in many places the opposition's chances of replacing the government were not rated very highly. If one ignores for the moment the fact that Krippendorff's arguments are very dependent on their historical context, a considerable amount of contradiction and lack of clarity is inherent in his theory as a whole. Why does he propagate effective inner-party democracy even though the governing party is capable of removing the opposition's basis for existence? Surely, within a party, the camp which makes use of the appropriate means of controlling possible crises would assert itself over the others. The author fails to make clear why opposition is superfluous whilst inner-party democracy is necessary.

As Krippendorff ignores the significance of elections and does not recognise the value of social pluralism, his analysis is not without its totalitarian aspects. Amongst other things, he makes the bold claim that in developing countries a single-party system has taken shape because of 'economic–administrative necessities', and 'a "democratic opposition party" is not only sociologi-

45. Ibid., pp. 69–70.
46. Hans-Peter Schneider, *Die parlamentarische Opposition im Verfassungsrecht der Bundesrepublik Deutschland*, vol. 1, Frankfurt/Main, 1974, p. 140. For a typical example of 'opposition pessimism' see Manfred Friedrich, *Opposition ohne Alternative?*, Cologne, 1962.

cally nonsensical, but politically, moreover, it represents a danger to the whole'. It is noticeable how Krippendorff, who teaches in Berlin, disputes the necessity for parliamentary opposition. Whilst he also warns of drawing superficial parallels, in his opinion 'the Soviet Union alone has anticipated the modern trend inherent in society towards a centralised one-party state – albeit at a high cost in human terms'.[47] This theory is based on a myth. The single-party dictatorship in the Soviet Union was imposed with violence and terror against the wishes of the majority of the population, whilst the tendencies in Western states towards 'single-party' systems, arguing purely from experience, result from the fact that the people's parties, according to the principle of the anticipated reaction, are oriented towards the interests and opinions of the citizens. Hence we are dealing with two facts as different as chalk and cheese.

Consequently, Krippendorff finds the concept of legitimate conflict which is regulated by elections unacceptable. According to him, the government should therefore view the existence of an opposition as a 'sign of its own socio-political mistakes'. His argument is not entirely clear when he considers that it belongs to the 'dialectics of historical development' that an opposition which achieves government should view its self-realisation as being 'to make any form of opposition socially unacceptable'. His observation that any tension in society can be 'removed by the alienation of consciousness',[48] is just as unclear. Obviously he cannot come to terms with the legitimate existence of a variety of differing interests. His theory that opposition becomes more impotent the more it adapts itself to the government is incorrect. In fact – at least in welfare states, upon which the author bases his theory – no opposition party which indulges in antiquated slogans and which promotes a revolutionary alternative to the ruling party will come to power.

How does Krippendorff justify his opinion that the 'end of the party state' is approaching? If he is correct in his socio-economic deduction that parties represent social classes, the reason is obvious. With the disappearance of class conflict in a welfare

47. Krippendorff, in *Der Monat*, 14.160/1962, pp. 68–9.
48. Ibid., pp. 67–9.

state, the parties would accordingly lose their function. In fact, however, there are numerous other areas of conflict (apart from political, ethical and religious ones, for example) which have led to the formation of parties. Krippendorff's theory is based on the single assumption that all serious political conflicts 'have their roots in economic factors'.[49]

Perhaps more important than criticism of Krippendorff's analysis for its narrow historical and empirical base is criticism of his inconsistency in using concepts which belong to a completely different political direction, the 'dialectics of historical development'. Just as Carl Schmitt considered the existence of parliamentarism in the nineteenth century as justified only because (apparently!) this was the only era when ideological bases functioned (i.e. access to the facts, discussion in the sense of seeking the truth), Krippendorff considers the party state to be the product of a passing phase, the first half of the twentieth century. Both suggest decay, but they measure certain changes unhistorically with measures which have been made absolute or are outdated.

Krippendorff understood the expression 'self-destruction', in relation to the party state, in Hegel's threefold sense – i.e. in the sense of *preserving, eliminating, improving*. All three interpretations are unfounded. In the first place, a single-party state such as the one Krippendorff has in mind can in no way retain the principles of a state under the rule of law and with a duty to protect minorities – to name but two principles. The election loses its meaning. Secondly, there is little to indicate the decline of the long-established party system – in spite of or perhaps because of the development of people's parties. On the whole, they make a change of government via elections easier. And the precarious development in many one-party states shows the virulence of oppositional forms of behaviour. Thirdly, the belief that the transformation to a one-party state brings about positive effects because of the 'effective realisation of inner-party democracy' but that this 'requires [!] more commitment'[50] is a purely personal one. Krippendorff claims that this would smooth the way for an enforced politicisation in favour of one direction.

49. Ibid., p. 68.
50. Ibid., p. 70.

Hence Krippendorff is correct neither in his diagnosis nor in his proposed 'therapy'.[51] Parliamentary opposition in the welfare states will not die out, and neither can their function – in a democratic political system – be replaced by other mechanisms. In many respects, the author has anticipated the arguments of the 'New Left', with whom he later associated himself. The implicit rejection of elections as an institutionalised mechanism for regulating conflict was obvious even then.

The 'New Left' intensified some of the elements of criticism which were hidden in Krippendorff's theory. This is particularly true of the view that elections serve to disguise, pacify and manipulate, thereby functioning as a purely formal democratic mechanism.[52] The criticism of elections advanced by the new social movements has much to do with perceptions developed in the second half of the 1960s.

While the criticism diagnoses various weaknesses of current electoral practice (for instance, the handling of an election campaign like an 'advertising campaign'), it comes nowhere near to presenting a convincing 'therapy'. Raschke's comment that elections in an 'enlightened'[53] society (whatever that may be) have a completely different function is just as unhelpful as Agnoli's Sibylline argument, which specifically rejects a theoretical alternative concept for elections and supports dubious voluntarism verging on the irresponsible:

> It is more important to experiment in the following areas: the practice of conflict, the autonomous efforts by workers to organise, new

51. Krippendorff repeated his theory in 1966: 'Ende des Parteienstaates?', *Die neue Gesellschaft*, 13/1962, pp. 3–10. The fact that the Labour Party replaced the Conservative government in Britain in 1964 in no way contradicts his theory, he claims, but at most relativises it, because the Labour Party was able to obtain a majority only after 'basically conducting class war' and thus had been able to mobilise dissatisfied voters. With this dialectic argument he even manages to pass off the British elections as 'an example confirming this theory of the party state' (ibid., p. 4–9).

52. See for example the criticisms in Johannes Agnoli, *Die Transformation der Demokratie*, Berlin, 1968; Wilfried Gottschalch, *Parlamentarismus und Rätedemokratie*, Berlin, 1968; Ursula Schmiederer, *Wahlen in der Bundesrepublik*, Frankfurt/Main, 1970; Wolf-Dieter Narr (ed.), *Auf dem Wege zum Einparteienstaat*, Opladen, 1977; Roland Roth (ed.), *Parlamentarisches Ritual und politische Alternativen*, Frankfurt/Main, 1980.

53. Raschke, in Steffani, *Parlamentarismus ohne Transparenz*, p. 198.

forms of self-organisation in the area of reproduction, and the movement of the dependent masses. In this way, the real limits to and direction in which social reform is possible can be determined, in forms which have nothing more to do with the old form of rule by representation.[54]

Narr and Vack's plea for 'new forms of expression of intention, co-determination and decision-making' is similarly vague – and also dangerous, because it obviously proposes instrumenting extra-parliamentary activities with the purpose of invalidating parliamentary majority decisions: 'It is advisable to take part in elections and to gain maximum benefit from them. But our demands go further than this and aim to achieve other forms of politics in order to make fundamental democracy possible in the first place.'[55]

However one evaluates this and other forms of criticism, there is no democratically based alternative to elections. They represent the most important form of 'institutionalised participation' (Dieter Nohlen) of the people, even though there are other forms of political participation (for example, membership of parties and associations, involvement in citizens' initiatives, participation in demonstrations) whose importance in all Western democracies has grown since the early 1970s, not least in West Germany, where 'new social movements' have had a considerable impact. For the citizen who is interested in political activity, the opportunity to influence political decisions is not limited to voting once every four years in the elections. On the other hand, the politically passive citizen is accommodated by the act of voting, which does not take up much time and involves little commitment. One should not view extra-parliamentary activity and parliamentary involvement as alternatives. The Green Party has gradually learnt that elections can in fact contribute to change. In short, the Western democracies are not progressing 'on the road to the one-party state' (Wolf-Dieter Narr).

54. Johannes Agnoli, 'Wahlkampf und sozialer Konflikt', in Narr, *Auf dem Wege zum Einparteienstaat*, p. 241.
55. Wolf-Dieter Narr and Klaus Vack, 'Glotzt nicht so wahlromantisch!', *Vorgänge*, 25.83/1986, pp. 127–8.

3
Elections, Electoral Systems and Parties in Selected States

The Range of Democratic Electoral Systems

Different democracies have different electoral systems, which in some cases are laid down in the constitution. The type of electoral system used in any given country is the result of a number of factors, including historical traditions, social structure, customary methods of controlling conflict, and the particular political culture.

The majority system is practised in the following member countries of the Organisation for Economic Co-operation and Development (OECD): the United States, Canada, New Zealand and the United Kingdom, which practise the relative-majority system; Australia and France, which use the absolute-majority system; and the Republic of Ireland and Japan, which have small constituencies with several seats (three to five). All the other OECD countries use proportional representation, though the specific form of organisation varies greatly. An electoral system intended to distribute seats in exact proportion to the votes cast does not exist. Limitation of the degree of proportionality occurs either by artificial barriers (restrictive clauses) or by natural barriers (due to the number of the seats available in a constituency). For example, in Sweden a party has to achieve at least 4% of the votes in order to participate in the distribution of seats. In Portugal, on the other hand, the success of a party depends on how many seats it gains in the constituencies, which are of varying sizes; the calculation of seats occurs separately in each constituency according to the d'Hondt 'highest-number system' (see below for details). Spain combines natural barriers with artificial ones. A party is only considered in the distribution of seats if it has gained at least 3% of the votes in the particular constituency.

The difference between the proportional representation systems with artificial barriers and those with natural barriers is that, in the former, all parties that have overcome the restrictive clause are allocated seats in proportion to their percentage of the votes, whilst, in the latter, the largest parties profit disproportionately from the effect of the restrictive clause in the constituency. The fewer the number of seats allocated in multi-seat constituencies, the truer this is. Some systems, like that in Greece, are more 'mixed', owing to the effect of multi-stage allocation processes in restricting proportionality. To a certain extent, Spain's electoral system also has a majority-forming effect, because it has some small constituencies in which, naturally, only large parties stand a chance.

If one wishes to limit proportionality (and this is the case everywhere), this can be effected by a national restrictive clause (*artificial barrier*) or by smaller multi-seat constituencies (*natural barriers*). In principle, an artificial barrier fulfils the restrictive function much better than a natural one. It is fairer because it favours all parties equally which have overcome the restrictive clause. The result of the election is easier to calculate, because there is a direct relation between the proportion of votes and the proportion of seats. Finally, the multi-seat constituency system can discourage the formation of majorities in parliament by distributing seats to small parties with a strong local base. On the other hand, it can give the largest party a blatant advantage. Incidentally, most countries have multi-seat constituencies rather than national restrictive clauses. The reason may lie in electoral dogma. An artificial barrier is seen as more drastic, even though the consequences for smaller multi-seat constituencies are the same.[1]

Classification according to type of electoral system is only one, albeit an essential, form of classification. If one classifies according to type of constituency, there are single-seat constituencies, multi-seat constituencies and national constituencies, but the type of constituency does not necessarily follow from the type of electoral system: for example, the United Kingdom, with its relative-majority system, has single-seat constituencies, and so has West Germany, where proportional representation is practised. The choice of candidate also varies considerably. With

1. For further details see the beginning of Chapter 4.

Table 3.1 Electoral systems, types of constituency and choice of party candidates in democracies

Constituency type	Choice of party candidates		
	None	Limited and ineffective in practice	Considerable
Single-seat constituencies	United Kingdom (RM) New Zealand (RM) Canada (RM) West Germany (PR)	Australia (AM) France (AM)	United States (RM with primaries)
Multi-seat constituencies	Spain (PR) Portugal (PR)	Belgium (PR) Austria (PR) Norway (PR) Sweden (PR)	Italy (PR) Denmark (PR) Finland (PR) Switzerland (PR) Luxembourg (PR) Ireland (M–STV)
Nationwide constituencies	Israel (PR)	Netherlands (PR)	

AM   = absolute-majority system
M–STV = majority system, single-transferable vote
PR   = proportional representation
RM   = relative-majority system

Source: Vernon Bogdanor (ed.), *Representatives of the People? Parliamentarians and Constituents in Western Democracies*, Cambridge, 1985, p. 11. Incidentally, the Irish electoral system is considered to be a majority system rather than proportional representation. The original table has been supplemented with several additional countries.

an inflexible list the voter is not left any leeway, whereas with a more flexible list he may change the order of the applicants. Ireland is a special case inasmuch as the voters may indicate preferences on the ballot sheet (by numbering the candidates in order of preference) and the transferability of votes is guaranteed if they have not yet been used to elect a candidate. This *single transferable vote*, which in British electoral research is wrongly interpreted as a separate electoral system, has no essential connection with either proportional representation or majority systems.[2] Table 3.1 summarises the three dimensions of electoral systems, types of constituencies and choice of candidates for various Western democracies. It not only shows how varied the existing rules are, but also demonstrates the lack of a straightforward connection between majority systems and election of individuals, on the one hand, and between proportional representation and voting for lists, on the other.

The following overview of the United Kingdom, France and West Germany is intended to highlight their differences, in terms both of historical development and of voting-rules. The discussion will also briefly consider differences in voting-behaviour.

The United Kingdom

According to Christian Graf van Krockow, reform differs from revolution 'not necessarily by the extent of change but by the fact that the basis for legitimacy of the existing order of rule either remains completely intact or is only changed gradually over a longer period of time'.[3] The accuracy of this definition is verified – indeed typified – by the example of the history of the franchise in the United Kingdom. The process of conversion from pre-democratic parliamentarism to parliamentary mass democracy occurred in the nineteenth and early twentieth centuries without any revolutionary, radical changes. The electoral reforms, which occurred gradually over a period of time, were one of the reasons why Britain was spared revolutions.[4] At the beginning of the nineteenth century, Parliament – and not just the House of Lords – was still dominated by an exclusive class consisting mainly of members of the nobility. Appointed on the

2. For details of the Irish electoral system cf. Dieter Nohlen, *Wahlrecht und Parteiensysteme*, Opladen, 1986, pp. 176–82; Peter Mair, 'Districting Choices under the Single-Transferable Vote', in Arend Lijphart and Bernard Grofman (eds), *Electoral Laws and their Political Consequences*, New York, 1986, pp. 289–307.
3. Christian Graf von Krockow, *Reform als politisches Prinzip*, Munich, 1976, p. 18.
4. For details see Hans Setzer, *Wahlsystem und Parteienentwicklung in England. Wege zur Demokratisierung der Institutionen 1832 bis 1948*, Frankfurt/Main, 1973; Franz Nuscheler, 'Großbritannien', in Dolf Sternberger and Bernhard Vogel (eds), *Die Wahl der Parlamente und anderer Staatsorgane. Ein Handbuch*, vol. 1: *Europa*, Berlin, 1969, pp. 605–50.

basis of a medieval electoral system which connected active and passive voting-rights with the ownership of property, the House of Commons came nowhere near to representing the population. Moreover, one could hardly talk of real elections. In the majority of cases, candidacy ensured the seat. Buying seats was an everyday occurrence, and trade in parliamentary seats was flourishing. Many small market towns which in the Middle Ages had been extremely important and had then been abandoned or had decayed ('rotten boroughs') still possessed seats which were occupied by influential property-owners. In a petition presented to the House of Commons in 1793, the blatant disparity of representation emerged: of the 558 members of Parliament in that year, seventy came from constituencies with no voters (!), ninety from constituencies with fewer than fifty voters, seventy from constituencies with fewer than 100 voters, and fifty-four from constituencies with fewer than 200 voters.[5] Hence several thousand voters elected over 50% of the members of the House of Commons. Booming industrial towns such as Birmingham and Manchester were not able to send any of their own representatives to Parliament. The total number of people eligible to vote was only approximately 450,000 (of a population of some 24 million).

The reform of 1832, which resulted mainly from pressure from the economically powerful bourgeoisie, who craved their own share of power, on the one hand extended the vote (particularly to the town-dwelling middle classes) and, on the other, abolished the worst distortions in the division into constituencies. Even though the immediate effects looked modest (a growth of the population eligible to vote from 0.5 million to 1 million[6]), it set in motion a process which gradually dismantled the privileges of the ruling classes. The period between the first (1832) and second (1867) reform bills is considered by many to be the 'classical period' of parliamentarism, because, they claim, this was when parliamentary sovereignty asserted itself. It is certainly true that this era saw far-reaching parliamentarisation of the political system, but the Crown still possessed a considerable

5. Cf. Iring Fetscher, *Politikwissenschaft*, Frankfurt/Main, 1968, p. 117.
6. For details of this and the following statements regarding the increase in the number of people eligible to vote cf. the table in Setzer, *Wahlsystem und Parteienentwicklung in England*, p. 271.

amount of power, especially as no pronounced party fronts had formed in Parliament, despite the existence of Whigs and Tories. No longer 'tied' to the Crown but not yet tied to parties, the MPs fulfilled their duties in a very slapdash manner. 'This inability to form a parliamentary majority was not an advantage, but a definite disadvantage, for the British system of government around the middle of the century.'[7]

Following the electoral reform of 1867, which the Conservatives put through under pressure from public opinion, the number of those eligible to vote rose by approximately 1 million. The reform benefited the middle classes, but town-dwelling workers whose annual rent equalled or exceeded the stipulated minimum also profited from it. The third major electoral reform, in 1884, extended the right to vote predominantly to agricultural workers and artisans (the estimated increase in those eligible to vote was around 2 million) and created constituencies which were of an approximately equal size and which were on the whole single-member constituencies. (Until then multi-member constituencies, particularly two-member constituencies, had predominated.) Electoral reform had ceased to spark off any massive controversies when in 1918 the franchise was extended to all adult men and to women over thirty who fulfilled certain property qualifications. This increased the electorate from approximately 8.4 to 21.4 million people. Universal suffrage for women was introduced in 1928. The democratisation of the vote was completed after the Second World War with the abolition of privileges for academics and the self-employed.

The only thing which today's Parliament has in common with the Parliament which existed at the beginning of the nineteenth century is its name. The change in structure implied by the progressive extension of the franchise was intensified by the development of the parties and the growing power and influence of the House of Commons. Nevertheless, this development cannot be termed a revolution. The bases of the rulers' legitimacy changed only gradually. As parliamentary mass democracy took shape, the importance of the House of Lords declined. In 1911 it lost its influence over financial legislation,

7. Adolf M. Birke, 'Die Souveränität des viktorianischen Parlaments und die moderne Parlamentarismuskritik', *Der Staat*, Supplement 1, Berlin, 1975, p. 73.

and its power to delay other bills was reduced to one year after the Second World War. Another venerable institution has experienced an even greater loss of power – the Crown: it must be completely neutral as far as party politics is concerned and must abide by the government's decisions. As a result it has a purely representative function, but, by symbolically personifying the unity of the country, it contributes to the integration of the population.

Britain is seen as the prototype of the two-party system. In the 1920s the Labour Party replaced the Liberals, who at times had been split into several camps, as the 'second force'. This was caused not least by the extension of the franchise in 1918 and 1928. The two-party system settled in (again). The Liberals no longer had any real significance. Since 1945, the two major parties have invariably won more than 95% of the seats.

In Britain, voting takes place according to the principle of relative majority, the original intention of which was that each constituency should be represented by one MP. Since then, however, a fundamental change has taken place, owing to the existence of national parties. In any constituency, the person who receives the most votes is elected. Elections must take place at intervals of no more than five years, and within that period the Prime Minister can dissolve Parliament at any time. Usually elections take place before the five-year period is over. If an MP leaves the House of Commons before a general election is called, a by-election is held for the seat. Incidentally, by-elections do not represent a mood barometer, because the candidate of the ruling party usually loses, or wins with a reduced majority. The personal element plays only a marginal role in elections, because the swing is uniform to an extraordinarily high degree. *Swing* means the number of percentage points by which the difference in support between the two major parties has changed. In recent years, this has shown a marked divergence from the average in constituencies where, for example, the election result promises to be very close. There is an increasing tendency for people in such marginal seats to vote tactically, so that, for example, a voter who normally supports Labour will vote for a third-party candidate if he thinks that that candidate has a better chance against the Conservative. Overall, the electoral turn-out is low (about 75%), and it is particularly low in constituencies where there is no doubt which candidate will win.

Characteristic of the British majority system is the so-called 'amplifying-effect', whereby a party without an overall majority of votes cast can win a majority of seats and so form a government without having to enter a coalition. In the thirteen general elections since 1945, no party has ever achieved a majority of votes, but only in the first election of 1974 did no party achieve an absolute majority of seats (see Table 3.2). The Conservative and Labour parties have had almost the same number of terms in office, though the Conservatives are ahead of Labour in terms of years in power. In the 1951 and February 1974 elections, the party with the largest number of votes did not have the largest number of seats, owing to the bias resulting from the concentration of its support in stronghold areas. In 1951 it was Labour that suffered from this effect; in February 1974, the Conservatives. In consequence, critics have described the outcome of British elections as a kind of gamble, but this is not quite true inasmuch as there used to be a certain pattern to the overall result: each party's share of seats was roughly equivalent to its share of votes after cubing the total votes received by each party. This *cubic rule*, identified by the Frenchman Poisson, has no longer applied since the 1970s, owing to the regionalisation of voting behaviour and a consequent drastic reduction in the number of marginal seats.[8]

The considerable difference between share of votes cast and share of seats won has long been generally approved by the British public opinion. However, since the 1970s, broad reform discussions have started: critics have arrived on the scene, suggestions for reform have been presented, commissions have been set up. The current electoral system has found and still finds few supporters[9] in academic literature. Supporters of the

8. See John Curtice and Michael Steed, 'Proportionality and Exaggeration in the British Electoral System', *Electoral Studies*, 5/1986, pp. 209–28.

9. See for example Vernon Bogdanor, *The People and the Party System: The Referendum and Electoral Reform in British Politics*, Cambridge, 1981, esp. pp. 175–260. The suggestions made by the Hansard Society, proposing an electoral system similar to that of West Germany, caused a great sensation; see Hansard Society for Parliamentary Government, *The Report of the Hansard Society Commission on Electoral Reform*, London, 1976. One of the few defences of the majority system can be found in Peter Hain, *Proportional Misrepresentation: The Case against PR in Britain*, Aldershot, 1986. Hain's argument is far from convincing. In this regard, see for example his criticism of the list electoral system

Table 3.2 United Kingdom: results of elections to the the House of Commons, 1922–87

Year	Ruling party	Conservatives			Labour			Liberal[a]		
		Votes %	Seats %	No.	Votes %	Seats %	No.	Votes %	Seats %	No.
1922	C	39.0	56.0	346	29.5	23.0	142	29.0	18.5	115
1923	L	38.0	42.0	258	30.5	31.0	191	29.5	26.0	159
1924	C	47.0	67.0	419	33.0	24.5	151	18.0	6.5	40
1929	L	38.0	42.0	260	37.0	47.0	288	23.5	10.0	59
1931	C+L	55.0	76.0	521	30.0	8.5	52	11.0	12.0	37
1935	C	54.0	70.0	431	37.5	25.0	154	6.5	3.0	21
1945	L	39.8	33.0	212	47.8	62.0	393	9.0	2.0	12
1950	L	43.5	47.8	298	46.1	50.4	315	9.1	1.5	9
1951	C	48.0	51.5	321	48.8	47.0	295	2.5	1.0	6
1955	C	49.7	54.6	344	46.4	43.9	277	2.7	1.0	6
1959	C	49.4	56.3	365	43.8	40.9	258	5.9	1.0	6
1964	L	43.4	48.2	304	44.1	50.3	317	11.2	1.5	9
1966	L	41.9	40.2	253	47.9	57.6	363	8.5	1.9	12
1970	C	46.4	52.4	330	43.0	45.5	287	7.5	1.0	6
1974(i)	L	38.1	46.8	297	37.2	47.4	301	19.3	2.2	14
1974(ii)	L	35.8	47.6	277	39.2	50.2	319	18.3	2.0	13
1979	C	43.9	53.4	339	37.0	42.4	269	13.8	1.7	11
1983	C	42.4	61.1	397	27.6	32.1	209	25.4	3.5	23
1987	C	42.2	57.8	376	30.1	35.2	229	22.6	3.4	22

(a) In the 1983 and 1987 elections the Liberal Party and Social Democractic Party fought a joint campaign as the 'Alliance'. Figures for those years represent the Alliance performance.
Source: amalgamated from various statistics.

majority system have been on the defensive, but the arguments against the traditional electoral system have come from opposing directions. One side denounces the injustice of the extreme disparity between share of votes and share of seats in a system where it is still possible to form a government without coalitions. The other side, by contrast, argues that the system no longer guarantees that a party will be able to gain an overall majority. The situation where this occurs is known as a 'hung parliament'. This 'pincer movement' working against the majority system could eventually lead to its abolition. Factors tending to increase the likelihood of a hung parliament include the fall in the number of marginal seats, the rise in support for centre parties and nationalist groups, and the increasing 'mobility' of the voter.[10] All this makes it more difficult in the long run for the strongest party to win a majority of seats.

Much may depend on the further development of the 'third force'. Beginning in the 1970s, the two major parties became increasingly polarised, as a result of a growing emphasis on ideology – a development that conflicts with the theoretical premise that a majority system has a moderating effect. This led in the past to Liberals becoming stronger. In the two 1974 elections they achieved almost 20% of the votes. In 1981 a moderate group split from the Labour Party and formed the Social Democratic Party (SDP), which stood together with the Liberals as the Alliance in 1983 and 1987. The Alliance achieved 25.4% of the vote in 1983 and 23.1% in 1987, but because of the majority system won only twenty-three seats in 1983 and twenty-two in the 1987 election. In 1983 the Labour Party, with 27.6% of the votes, gained almost ten times as many seats as the Alliance. Following the 1987 election, special Liberal and SDP party congresses agreed, against the wishes of the charismatic SDP leader David Owen, to a fusion of the two parties in 1988.

(p. 15f.) and, in particular, his criticism of the West German electoral system, where he uncritically reproduces the Hansard Society's objections to 'two types of MPs' (p. 17). For a summary of the reform debate, see Vernon Bogdanor, 'Literature, Sources and Methodology for the Study of Electoral Reform in the United Kingdom', in Serge Noiret (ed.), *Stratégies politiques et réformes électorales: aux origines des modes de scrutin en Europe aux XIXème et XXème siècles*, Baden-Baden, 1990.

10. On this and other factors see David Butler, 'Electoral Reform and Political Strategy in Britain', ibid.

(Owen continued to lead a rump SDP until declining member-ship forced its dissolution in May 1990.) If the new Social and Liberal Democratic Party (SLDP) can overcome its initial difficul-ties and if the tendency towards ideologisation (which has admittedly been somewhat weakened recently) continues in the two other parties, then David Butler could be right with his prediction: 'it seems to me unlikely that first-past-the-post vot-ing for the Westminster Parliament will last to the end of the century'.[11] Given the fact that the British people have developed a greater need to participate in politics, this prediction seems, at the least, more plausible than the theory that the situation in Britain today resembles that in the 1920s. The dissolution of the Labour Party is not on the agenda, because support for the Alliance/SLDP has developed mainly in Conservative areas. In the 1983 general election, the Alliance candidate was in second place in 311 constituencies, of which the Conservatives won 263.[12] Further successes of the 'centre parties' may occur at the cost of the Conservatives. If a situation were to arise where these parties were needed to help form a government, they would probably only do so at the price of a change in the electoral system towards greater proportionality.

However in the European elections in 1989, the newly merged Social and Liberal Democrats received only a few per cent of the votes – a very disappointing result for their new leader, Paddy Ashdown – and were forced into fourth place behind a surpris-ingly successful Green Party (15%). Although retaining some of its former support in local government elections, the SLDP has received no encouragement from recent by-elections or opinion-poll results. The SLDP appears unlikely to prevent the Conser-vatives or Labour from once again obtaining a single-party majority of seats at the next general election.

In four of the last five general elections, less than 75% of the votes have gone to the two major parties – and that under the conditions of the first-past-the-post system! This is surprising because votes for the other parties generally end up going to waste. Voting-behaviour has also undergone massive changes

11. David Butler, 'Reflections on the Electoral Debate in Britain', in Lijphart and Grofman, *Electoral Laws*, p. 229.
12. See Vernon Bogdanor, 'Electoral Reform and British Politics', *Electoral Studies*, 6/1987, p. 116.

in other respects: the regionalisation of voting-behaviour is very advanced. The Labour Party increasingly has its strongholds in the structurally weak North, whilst the Conservatives can consider the South as their fortress. The SLDP constituency has a less specific character. In Wales and Scotland Labour is dominant, competing with nationalist groups who strive for greater autonomy from England.

France

If the development of the electoral system in Britain has been characterised by continuity, in France the process has been less straightforward. The French Revolution of 1789 sparked off far-reaching changes, and not just in France. The Assemblée Nationale, which comprised the selected representatives of the bourgeoisie, the third class, proclaimed human and civil rights. Consequently, a number of electoral laws were passed[13] which envisaged a vote restricted to people who paid taxes, whereby the qualifying conditions could be changed. During the Napeoleonic era and the restoration period, however, the bourgeoisie did not really participate effectively in political decision-making. The February revolution of 1848 resulted in the summoning of an assembly to decide on the constitution, which established universal suffrage for men. Continual changes in the electoral system were to characterise the following period, and indeed have continued right up to the present day, although universal suffrage, apart from a few short periods, has remained intact. The following systems have all existed at one time or another: a relative-majority system in both multi-seat and single-seat constituencies and an absolute-majority system in both multi-seat and single-seat constituencies. Proportional representation has also been practised at times (in the Fourth Republic from 1945 to 1958 – although elements of the majority system continued to exist – and then again in 1986).

However, the absolute-majority system of the Roman type has been used most frequently. To be voted into the Assemblée

13. For the historical background see Gisela Medzeg and Dieter Nohlen, 'Frankreich', in: Sternberger and Vogel, *Die Wahl der Parlamente*, Vol. 1, pp. 441–554.

Nationale in the first ballot, a candidate has to achieve an absolute majority of votes in his constituency. Otherwise a second ballot must take place in which the relative majority is the decisive factor. This electoral system encourages election alliances. It was also reintroduced in 1958 at the beginning of the Fifth Republic, mainly because proportional representation, as practised during the Fourth Republic, had caused continual instability – in the mid-1950s the authoritarian–populist movement of Poujadism experienced temporary success. In the 1958 election, the Gaullists gained over 40% of the seats with approximately 20% of the votes in the first ballot, whilst the Communists with almost 20% of the votes were only able to gain 2.1% of the seats because they did not have any alliance partners (see Table 3.3). It is true that the disproportional effects were not always this crass; however, they were only rarely adjusted.[14] Originally, all candidates who had achieved at least 5% of the votes in any one constituency were allowed to participate in the second ballot, but since 1966 they must win the support of at least 10% of the total number of people entitled to vote. This ruling is also responsible for the fact that increasingly fewer candidates are competing in the second ballot.

A bipolar party system began to form because the two major party blocks each agreed on one candidate in the second ballot. One of the reasons why this was possible was that the Parti Communiste Français (PCF) was largely successful in breaking out of the isolation it had experienced in the 1950s and 1960s. Incidentally, it was seen that, in the second ballot, support from Socialist voters crumbled in places where Communists were standing for election, and hence inter-party co-operation at voter level was not entirely successful. This also explains why the Communist Party, which is still (or again) seen as extremist in certain sectors, wins a considerably smaller share of seats than of votes. Perhaps the main reason for the bipolarity is the fact that the President is elected directly, following the constitutional reform of 1962. This occurs by means of an absolute-majority

14. For numerous examples and conversions see Byron Criddle, 'Distorted Representation in France', *Parliamentary Affairs*, 28/1975, pp. 154–79; David Goldey and Philip Williams, 'France', in Vernon Bogdanor and David Butler (eds), *Democracy and Elections: Electoral Systems and their Political Consequences*, Cambridge, 1983, pp. 62–83.

Table 3.3 France: results of elections to the Assemblée Nationale, 1958–88

	1958		1962		1967		1968		1973		1978		1981		1986		1988	
	votes %	seats %	votes %	seats %	votes %	seats %	votes %	seats %	votes %	seats %	votes %	seats %	votes %	seats %	votes %	seats %	votes %	seats %
Extreme left	0.9	–	2.0	0.4	2.2	0.8	3.9	–	3.3	0.6	3.3	0.2	1.3	–	1.5	–	0.4	–
Communists	18.9	2.1	21.9	8.6	22.5	15.3	20.0	7.0	21.3	15.0	20.6	17.5	16.2	9.0	9.8	6.1	11.3	4.7
Socialists	15.7	8.6	12.7	14.0	19.3	24.9	16.6	12.1	17.7	18.2	22.6	20.9	37.5	54.9	31.6	36.9	37.6	48.0
Left-wing radicals									1.4	2.5	2.1	2.0		2.9				
Radicals	8.2	8.0	5.8	8.4	15.4	9.4	12.5	6.6	12.6	6.4								
Centre	10.8	11.8	8.2	6.7					3.8	4.7	23.9	28.7	19.2	12.4	41.0	48.7	18.5	22.6
Republicans			[4.4]		[8.9]		[13.0]		7.0	11.1					[26.3]		19.2	22.3
Gaullists	20.3	42.2	35.5	55.0	38.3	49.6	46.4	74.3	24.0	37.7	22.6	30.1	20.8	17.3				
Extreme right	1.0	–	0.3	–			0.6	–			[1.8]		0.4	–	9.9	6.1	9.8	0.2
Independent	24.2	27.3	13.6	6.9	2.3	–			8.9	3.9	4.5	0.4	4.6	2.2	6.2	1.6	3.2	–
Others	–	–	–	–	–	–	–	–	–	–	–	–	–	–	–	–	–	–

The table simplifies events due to the party fluctuation which has occurred. The braces indicate groups which stood for election together. The square brackets indicate the strength of a particular group whose result has already been included in the overall result of the alliance. The statistics given for votes refer to the first ballot. In 1986, there was only one ballot, as in this year a system of proportional representation was used.

Source: Dieter Menyesch and Henrik Uterwedde, *Frankreich. Wirtschaft–Gesellschaft–Politik*, Opladen, 1982, pp. 174–6. The figures for the 1986 and 1988 elections were supplied by Henrik Uterwedde.

system (only the two candidates with the most votes are allowed to stand in the second ballot) and, due to the semi-presidential system of government, the presidential election is more important than elections for the Assemblée Nationale. Whilst in 1965 (de Gaulle), 1969 (Pompidou) and 1974 (Giscard d'Estaing) candidates from the 'Right' were able to win, in 1981 it was a Socialist, Mitterrand, who conquered his opponent from the Independent Republicans (Giscard d'Estaing). He was able to repeat his success in spring 1988 – this time against the Neo-Gaullist Chirac – which was less surprising than the high number of votes received by Le Pen, the extreme-right candidate, who gained 14.4% of the votes in the first ballot.

In 1981, for the first time in the Fifth Republic, the Parti Socialiste (PS) with its partner the Mouvement Radical de Gauche (MRG) achieved a majority in the Assemblée Nationale. At the end of the legislative period proportional representation was introduced, either because this had long been a Socialist demand (the left-wing parties in any case saw themselves as disadvantaged by the absolute-majority system, owing to the division of the electorate into constituencies), or because the Socialists, whose coalition with the Communists collapsed in 1984, feared that under the majority system this would spell their defeat in the next election, or because they hoped that Le Pen's extreme right would take votes from the middle right. Admittedly, a number of provisos were attached to the system of proportional representation, preventing a direct correlation (which was not desired) between share of votes and share of seats. The 96 multi-seat constituencies which were formed in 1986 were of varying sizes. In 60 of the constituencies two to five seats were allocated (total 204), in nine, 10–13 seats (total 103) and in five, 14–24 seats (total 89).[15] Hence, because of the constituencies, some of which were small, this electoral system did not result in a high degree of proportionality, and even in the large constituencies proportionality was limited. The parties had to achieve at least 5 per cent of the votes in the constituencies in order to participate in the allocation of seats.

Because of changes to the electoral system, the defeat of the

15. Cf. Andrew Knapp, 'Proportional but Bipolar: France's Electoral System in 1986', *West European Politics*, 10/1987, p. 94; Andrew Knapp, 'Orderly Retreat: Mitterrand Chooses PR', *Electoral Studies*, 4/1985, p. 257.

Socialists was less severe than it would otherwise have been: the Union pour la Démocratie Française (UDF) and the Neo-Gaullist Rassemblement pour la République (RPR), who, in spite of proportional representation, had previously committed themselves to an alliance in order to prevent fragmentation, achieved a 'breathtakingly narrow'[16] majority of seats together with diverse right-wing 'splinter groups', because the Le Pen movement (Front Nationale), which was seen as right-wing extremist, was able to gain 10% of the votes. The extreme right would not have been so successful under the conditions of the absolute-majority system.

As Table 3.3 shows, in 1986 the middle right gained only 41% of the votes, whilst the PS–MRG alliance achieved 32%; these figures translated into 49% and 37% of seats, respectively. The Communists, who were not available for an alliance with the Socialists this time, gained (like the Front Nationale) approximately 10% of the votes but only approximately 6% of the seats. This electoral system, then, also had a majority-forming effect, albeit limited, whereas in a pure proportional representation system neither of the main alliances would have been able to achieve a majority in the Assemblée Nationale. It is difficult to ascertain whether the limited proportional representation system did anything to reduce bipolarity. Approximately 10% of votes on both the left and the right of the political spectrum were for a party which was not prepared to join a coalition. After the election the (middle-class) majority immediately reintroduced the absolute-majority system.

The March 1986 election is interesting also for another reason. It is well-known that France has a semi-presidential system of government. For the first time in the Fifth Republic, the President, who is elected directly by the people, found himself having to work with a government formed from the opposing camp. The Socialist Mitterrand had to appoint the Gaullist Jacques Chirac as Prime Minister. So far this cohabitation has not caused as much conflict as was originally expected and has

16. Karlheinz Reif, 'Parlamentswahlen in Frankreich 1986: Neues Wahlrecht, neue Partei, neue Koalitionsmuster', *Zeitschrift für Parlamentsfragen*, 17/1986, p. 487.

led to a certain equilibrium.[17] This has continued since Mitterrand's victory in 1988.

In 1950 the French political scientist Maurice Duverger formulated a set of 'laws' on the connections between electoral systems and party systems,[18] and these have been taken up again and again. The interesting thing here is not so much his theories regarding proportional representation (that it encourages a party system with many parties and rigid fronts) or regarding the relative-majority system (that it encourages party dualism), but what he has to say regarding the absolute-majority system, because his theories about it are based principally on France. According to Duverger, the absolute-majority system encourages a party system with several parties and flexible fronts. Empirically, so far as France is concerned, this claim can be seen to be disproved, even though the party system changed primarily because of the presidential elections. For the foreseeable future, the bipolar party system seems destined to remain – provided that a return to proportional representation, which could break up the main party blocks, fails to materialise. Where France is concerned, one can never be sure.[19]

Nohlen has succinctly described the French perception of the electoral system as a 'formula for power', and Sternberger has stated this ironic paradox:

In almost one and a half centuries [since the February revolution], the French have become so used to this game between their oligarchies of party and parliament that they would perceive constancy

17. For a more optimistic view of future developments see Udo Kempf, 'Die "Cohabitation": Entmachtung des Präsidenten oder wiedergewonnenes Gleichgewicht?', *Zeitschrift für Parlamentsfragen*, 17/1986, pp. 502–15. A rather more sceptical view is presented in Adolf Kimmel, 'Der "Machtwechsel" von 1981 und die Entwicklung des politischen Systems der V. Republik', *Zeitschrift für Politik*, 34/1987, pp. 1–17.
18. See Maurice Duverger, 'Der Einfluß der Wahlsysteme auf das politische Leben' (1950), in Otto Büsch and Peter Steinbach (eds), *Vergleichende europäische Wahlgeschichte. Eine Anthologie. Beiträge zur historischen Wahlforschung vornehmlich West– und Nordeuropas*, Berlin, 1983, pp. 30–84.
19. On the discussion in France regarding literature, history and the current reform debate surrounding the electoral system, see the following articles in Noiret, *Strategies politiques et réformes électorales*: Claude Emeri, 'Les lois électorales en France: sources et historiographie'; René Remond, 'Les réformes électorales en France aux XIXe et XXe siècles'; Daniel Gaxie, 'Les partis politiques et les modes de scrutin en France (1985–1986): croyances et intérêts'.

as a break with legitimacy. Perhaps the relative sincerity in openly stating their motives contributes towards making the unacceptable behaviour of politicians more bearable.[20]

In this way there is still a positive side to the parties' Machiavellian strivings, but in the long run, by perpetually playing with the structure of the electoral system, the French are playing with fire, because this undermines the legitimacy of the order, even if in France loyalty is primarily to the nation and the republic. As a result, the constitution and the electoral system do not enjoy the same status as in West Germany.

Germany

The revolutionary events in France in 1848 soon spread to Germany, after a weak form of constitutionalism had previously appeared in only a few southern states within the German alliance. In order to avoid worse upheavals, the princes relinquished their power and appointed liberal ministers (so-called *Märzminister*). A parliamentary convention which emerged from the revolutionary movements determined the basic principles for elections to the national parliament which was to pass the constitution. The first German parliament, which had been desired by large sectors of the bourgeoisie, was elected partly by means of universal suffrage (for men). The constitution prescribed universal suffrage for elections to the lower house, but the counter-revolutionary forces, which had recovered from their temporary weakness, caused the revolution to fail.

Nevertheless, the work of the Frankfurt MPs laid the foundation stone for the further development of parliamentary democracy. From this time on, the two concepts of unity and freedom went in different directions. Otto von Bismarck capitalised on the trend towards unity and in 1866, following the war between Prussia and Austria, created the North German Confederation, from which the German Empire was formed in 1871, by annexing southern German states. Hence national

20. Nohlen, *Wahlrecht und Parteiensystem*, p. 140; Dolf Sternberger, *Grund und Abgrund der Macht. Über Legitimität von Regierungen*, new edn with 15 chs, Frankfurt/Main, 1986, p. 348.

unity was the achievement of the princes and the military. The new constitution retained an authoritarian tinge: the Reichstag (Imperial Parliament) could neither appoint the Reich Chancellor (Reichskanzler) nor overthrow him. The Chancellor did not have to answer to the Reichstag and depended much more on the trust of the Emperor, although he increasingly needed the support of parliament as well. The Reichstag shared legislative powers with the Bundesrat (Federal Council), the body representing the Länder (provinces). Amendments to the constitution could not be introduced if fourteen members of the Bundesrat voted against them. Hence any fundamental democratic constitutional reform was doomed to fail, because in Prussia, which possessed seventeen of the fifty-eight votes, democratic forces were clearly in the minority. The Prussian lower house was elected according to the 'three-class voting-system', which divided the population into three tax groups, each of which had to contribute one-third of the taxes. This vote, which moreover was neither secret nor direct, hardly disturbed the monarchic principle. Although frequently demanded, parliamentarisation of the governmental system did not occur until 1918.

In contrast to most other states at that time, the German Empire had at least established universal and equal suffrage for men, which it had taken over from the North German Confederation. The introduction of universal suffrage, which strengthened support for the Empire, was a tactical move by Bismarck, whose calculation – he was counting on the loyalty to authority of the rural population, whom he considered conservative – proved to be only partly correct.

Elections (initially once every three years and from 1888 once every five years) took place according to an absolute-majority system in single-seat constituencies. If no one received the absolute majority in the first ballot, a second ballot took place between the two most successful candidates. No adjustment of constituency boundaries occurred until 1918, though the growth in the population and migration from the country to the towns had long since produced considerable disparity in the size of constituencies. The Conservatives profited from this 'passive constituency democracy', which had a particularly detrimental effect on the Social Democrats. So did the second-ballot system:

Table 3.4 Germany: results of elections to the Reichstag, 1871–1912

Year	Turn-out %	Social Democrats %	Left- wing liberal %	Zentrum %	Right- wing liberal %	Conserva- tives %	Minorities/ regional groups %
1871	52.0	3.1	9.3	18.7	37.2	23.1	6.6
1874	61.2	6.8	9.0	27.9	30.8	14.2	10.5
1877	61.6	9.1	8.6	25.0	29.7	17.6	9.8
1878	63.4	7.6	7.9	23.1	25.8	26.7	8.9
1881	56.3	6.1	22.9	23.2	15.0	23.7	8.8
1884	60.5	9.7	19.3	22.6	17.6	22.1	8.5
1887	77.5	10.1	14.1	20.1	22.6	25.1	7.7
1890	71.5	19.7	18.2	18.6	16.8	19.8	6.6
1893	72.4	23.3	14.3	19.1	13.2	22.8	7.1
1898	68.1	27.2	11.8	18.8	13.1	20.8	8.1
1903	76.1	31.7	9.5	19.5	14.2	17.4	7.1
1907	84.7	28.9	11.4	19.4	14.7	18.1	6.6
1912	84.2	34.8	12.8	16.4	14.1	15.3	6.3

Source: Alfred Milatz, 'Reichstagswahlen und Mandatverteilung 1871 bis 1918', in Gerhard A. Ritter (ed.), *Gesellschaft, Parlament und Regierung. Zur Geschichte des Parlamentarismus in Deutschland*, Düsseldorf, 1974, p. 220f.

in the second ballot the middle-class parties frequently made election pacts to defeat the Social Democratic candidate, where he was in the lead after the first ballot. This also distorted the relationship between share of votes and share of seats.[21] As early as 1890 the Social Democrats, who in contrast to other parties stood for election almost everywhere, were the party with the most votes, but it was not until 1912 that they became the party with the most seats.

In spite of the majority system, five major camps formed in the Reichstag (see Table 3.4). The Conservatives tried to retain their privileges. Whilst the Deutschkonservativen (German Conservatives) mourned the passing of the feudal system, the less significant Freikonservativen (Free Conservatives) were also involved in organising industrialists. The liberal right wing, in the form of the Nationalliberalen (National Liberals), were

21. For further details see Hans Fenske, *Wahlrecht und Parteiensystem. Ein Beitrag zur deutschen Parteiengeschichte*, Frankfurt/Main, 1972, pp. 106–45; Alfred Milatz, 'Reichtagswahlen und Mandatsverteilung 1871 bis 1918. Ein Beitrag zu Problemen des absoluten Mehrheitswahlrechts', in Gerhard A. Ritter (ed.), *Gesellschaft, Parlament und Regierung. Zur Geschichte des Parlamentarismus in Deutschland*, Düsseldorf, 1974, pp. 207–23.

largely in favour of a powerful (Bismarckian) state and a constitutional monarchy; the liberal left, on the other hand, which was split into several parties, led by the Fortschrittspartei (Progressive Party), supported a parliamentary monarchy modelled on Great Britain. The Zentrum (Centre), held together by the Catholic faith, combined employers', farmers' and workers' interests. Sozialdemokratie (Social Democracy) occupied a special position because its opponents associated it with 'anti-patriotic forces'; it was only integrated into the state very slowly.

Efforts towards a reform of electoral rights, particularly by the Social Democrats, did not bring any success. It was not until August 1918 that it was decided to calculate seats (from two to ten) according to the principle of proportionality, and then only in certain constituencies with a mainly urban population. The Social Democrats unwaveringly propagated proportional representation – partly because this method reduced their disadvantage, and partly out of consideration for the principle of equality. Hence it was not surprising that, following the collapse of the old order, the Council of People's Representatives, consisting of representatives from the SPD and USPD (for explanation of abbreviations see Table 3.5), announced the introduction of elections according to a system of proportional representation. The new democracy, which was confronted with numerous endurance tests from the very beginning, created a constitution which was entirely based on the principle of people's sovereignty and which aimed to introduce plebiscitary elements such as referenda and popular election of the president. The constitution could be changed at will, provided that the necessary majority was in favour. The liberal optimism of the fathers of the constitution was unlimited, and it was not considered necessary to take any precautions to protect the constitution.

The electoral law fitted smoothly into this concept of democracy.[22] The ordinance providing for elections to the national assembly envisaged thirty-six large constituencies, in which between six and seventeen seats would be allocated according to the D'Hondt 'highest-number system', and the electoral law

22. See Eberhard Schanbacher, *Parlamentarische Wahlen und Wahlsystem in der Weimarer Republik. Wahlgesetzgebung und Wahlreform im Reich und in den Ländern*, Düsseldorf, 1982, pp. 66–89.

passed by the Reichstag further perfected the principle of proportional representation. The allocation of seats occurred in
three stages: in the first phase, the parties received a seat for
every 60,000 votes in any of the thirty-five constituencies (the
actual number created); in the second phase, further seats were
created by the excess votes at the level of the seventeen constituency groupings; in the third and final phase, the parties once
again received one seat from their national list for every 60,000
votes, and one seat per 30,000 for the remaining votes. A party
which failed to gain 60,000 votes in any constituency did not
receive any seats even if it exceeded this quorum many times
over in the country as a whole. Moreover, a party could not be
allotted more seats from its national list than it had received at
constituency and constituency-grouping level. Although this
did not mean, as is often thought, that most seats were based on
60,000 votes, nevertheless the opportunities for smaller parties
were extremely favourable.

Despite numerous efforts towards further electoral reform,
the system described above was not changed, apart from a few
technical modifications, till the fall of the Weimar Republic.
Prior to that, political and, above all, academic reform proposals
were concerned less with the abolition of proportional representation (other than to exclude the smallest parties) than with
supplementing or even totally replacing the list election with
personal elements (for instance, by enlarging the number of
constituencies). This was the key issue in most suggestions.

The party system of the German Empire continued during the
Weimar Republic within certain limitations, and initially
voting-behaviour did not reveal any serious differences. However, this soon changed (see Table 3.5): the DNVP (which
consisted mainly of supporters of the Conservative parties of the
German Empire), the KPD (which had emerged from the left
wing of the USPD, which was soon to split up) and the NSDAP
(Nazi Party), which had formed from nationalist groups and
which combined fanatical anti-semitism with anti-bolshevism,
campaigned against the Weimar Republic. Regardless of the
outcome of elections, the Zentrum and the (left-liberal) DDP
participated as centre parties in almost all of the (generally
complicated) governments formed during this period. There
was no adequate working majority, for the 75% majority

Table 3.5 Germany: results of elections to the Reichstag, 1919–33

Year	Turn-out %	KPD %	USPD %	SPD %	DDP %	Zentrum %	BVP %	DVP %	DNVP %	NSDAP %	Others %
1919	83.0	–	7.6	37.9	18.5	19.7	–	4.4	10.3	–	1.6
1920	79.2	2.1	17.9	21.7	8.3	13.6	4.4	13.9	15.1	–	4.0
1924 (May)	77.4	12.6	0.8	20.5	5.7	13.4	3.2	9.2	19.5	6.5	8.6
1924 (Dec)	78.6	9.0	0.3	26.0	6.3	13.6	3.7	10.1	20.5	3.0	7.5
1928	75.6	10.6	0.1	29.8	4.9	12.1	3.1	8.7	14.2	2.6	13.9
1930	82.0	13.1	–	24.5	3.8	11.8	3.0	4.5	7.0	18.3	14.0
1932 (July)	84.1	14.3	–	21.6	1.0	12.5	3.2	1.2	5.9	37.3	3.0
1932 (Nov)	80.6	16.9	–	20.4	1.0	11.9	3.1	1.9	8.3	33.1	3.4
1933 (Mar)	88.8	12.3	–	18.3	0.9	11.2	2.7	1.1	8.0	43.9	1.6

BVP   Bayerische Volkspartei (Bavarian People's Party)
DDP   Deutsche Demokratische Partei (German Democratic Party)
DNVP   Deutschnationale Volkspartei (German National People's Party)
DVP   Deutsche Volkspartei (German People's Party)
KPD   Kommunistische Partei Deutschlands (Communist Party of Germany)
NSDAP   Nationalsozialistische Deutsche Arbeiterpartei (National Socialist German Workers' Party)
SPD   Sozialdemokratische Partei Deutschlands (Social Democratic Party of Germany)
USPD   Unabhängige Sozialistische Partei Deutschlands (Independent Socialist Party of Germany)

Source: Bernhard Vogel, Dieter Nohlen and Rainer-Olaf Schulze, *Wahlen in Deutschland. Theorie–Geschichte–Dokumente 1848–1970*, Berlin, 1970, p. 296ff.

achieved by the Weimar Coalition in 1919 (SPD, Zentrum, DDP) was merely a 'nine-day wonder'. The union-oriented SPD and the DVP, which was hostile to the unions, were divided by deep, almost irreconcilable conflict. Hence a negative parliamentarism was increasingly characteristic of political development: parliamentary majorities were capable of overthrowing governments but not usually capable of working together constructively, especially as it was an almost everyday occurrence for the coalition to collapse (least so during the period 1924–8). No government survived its full appointed term of office.

In the final phase of the Weimar democracy, the influence of the Reichstag, which in any case was not excessively strong, shrank even further through the formation of presidential cabinets. Since 1932 the extremist forces of the right and the left had formed a 'negative majority'. When Hitler, whose NSDAP had completely wiped out political liberalism, was appointed Chancellor by the aged President Paul von Hindenburg, that was marked the end of democracy. Elections in the 'Third Reich' only served to confirm decisions which had already been made, although in an election with competing parties the National Socialist system would probably have been approved (if only temporarily) by the majority of the population, owing to the improvement it had made to the economic situation, its foreign-policy successes and the international reputation it enjoyed. However, a government is not legitimised simply because 'the entirety of the unit, or the vast majority, is convinced that "the people" determine their own destiny and that the government is working for its good and not for that of a minority, elite, etc.'[23]

After 1945, a violent dispute erupted, which is still continuing today, as to whether and to what extent the system of pure proportional representation led to the demise of the Weimar Republic or at least accelerated it. Supporters of this theory cite the following factors in support of their argument: party fragmentation, which favours extreme pluralism, encourages disintegration and does nothing to control increasing radicalism; the impersonal list election, which tends to diminish the represen-

23. John H. Herz, 'Gedanken über Legalität, Gewalt und die Zukunft des Staates', in: Christian Fenner and Bernhard Blanke (eds), *Systemwandel und Demokratisierung*, Frankfurt/Main, 1975, p. 37f. Herz's attempt at a definition comprises a necessary – but by no means adequate – condition for legitimacy.

tatives' sense of commitment; and inadequate institutional rules to combat fringe parties. Critics of the theory object that its proponents attribute exaggerated importance to the electoral system and fail to appreciate that a large number of factors were responsible for the collapse of the Weimar democracy. The party structure, they argue, would hardly have been fundamentally changed by a majority voting-system.

These arguments are difficult to disprove. Moreover, it was not so much the large number of parties which crippled the Weimar democracy as the fact that the major parties were unwilling to form a coalition. Above all, however, those who argue that a majority system would have worked better over-look the fact that the option of introducing this electoral system was not seriously discussed in the Weimar Republic.

The Basic Law of the Federal Republic draws many con-clusions from painful historical experience, but less so in the case of the electoral system. Admittedly, this time the electoral system was not anchored in the constitution, in order to make changing it easier, but those who repeatedly recalled the Wei-mar experiences in Bundestag debates were not able to realise their demands for a majority system. However, the much-criticised anonymous list of the Weimar Republic was rectified – at least in part – by pre-selection of candidates and the creation of single-seat constituencies; and party fragmentation was pre-vented by the restrictive clause. Paradoxically, the supporters of proportional representation were much more vociferous than their opponents in citing the Weimar experiences to show what should not be allowed to happen.

In the German Democratic Republic, developments were quite different. In April 1946 the East German KPD and SPD were compelled to merge to form the Sozialistische Einheits-partei Deutschlands (Socialist Unity Party of Germany, SED), which controlled East German political life until the revolution-ary events of autumn 1989. The five parties – the SED, the Christlich Demokratische Union (Christian Democratic Union), the Liberal-demokratische Partei Deutschlands (Liberal Demo-cratic Party of Germany), the National-demokratische Partei Deutschlands (National Democratic Party of Germany) and the Demokratische Bauernpartei Deutschlands (Democratic Peasants' Party of Germany) – and five mass organisations (for example,

Table 3.6 GDR: results of elections to the Volkskammer, 1950–86

	Turn-out (%)	Yes votes (%)
1950	98.53	99.72
1954	98.51	99.46
1958	98.90	99.87
1963	99.25	99.95
1967	98.82	99.93
1971	98.48	99.85
1976	98.58	99.86
1981	99.21	99.86
1986	99.74	99.94

Source: compiled from the statistical yearbooks of the GDR.

the Freier Deutscher Gewerkschaftsbund – the Free German Trade Union Federation) combined to form the Nationale Front der Deutschen Demokratischen Republik, which made up the unified list of candidates for elections. Seats in the Volkskammer (People's Chamber), the highest representative body of the people in the GDR, were allocated to the individual factions according to a predetermined, fixed pattern. The 1972 abortion bill, which produced fourteen votes against and eight abstentions, was an exceptional case. Elections, which were preceded by a 'socialist election movement' – the candidates were supposed to justify themselves in answer to any question at the election meetings and 'discussions' – did not have any significance for the 'power question'. Electoral turn-out was always over 98%, and the number of yes votes always well over 99% (see Table 3.6). People who actually used the voting-booths laid themselves open to the suspicion that they did not trust the candidates. The most important aspects of the principle of 'freedom of election' were not taken into account.[24] Beginning in 1981, MPs in the East Berlin Volkskammer were directly elected, which contravened Berlin's four-power status.

The revolutionary upheaval of autumn 1989,which took professional observers completely by surprise, changed the situation in the GDR abruptly and completely. Under pressure from

24. Cf. Peter J. Lapp, *Wahlen in der DDR*, Berlin, 1982. For a GDR viewpoint see Herbert Graf and Günter Seiler, *Wahl und Wahlrecht in Klassenkampf*, Berlin (East), 1971, pp. 149–268.

the increasing exodus of GDR citizens to the West, and the opposition movements that suddenly emerged, the communist system of Erich Honecker broke down with little resistance. The border with the Federal Republic was opened. New parties quickly formed and old ones severed their links with the SED, which in 1990 changed its name to the Partei Demokratischer Sozialismus (Party of Democratic Socialism). The transitional government prepared itself for democratic elections. On 18 March 1990 the first democratic elections in the GDR took place. As expected, the majority of East Germans repudiated the communist party (16.3%) and therewith signalled the end of the GDR. A union of the two German states should now be just a matter of time.

Comparison and Summary

This brief historical overview of parties, parliamentary democracy and elections in the United Kingdom, France and Germany has illustrated the very different courses of development of their electoral systems. Admittedly they also have some things in common. In all three countries a bipolar party system has developed, regardless of the specific electoral system, and in all cases, despite the major differences, the rules include provisos aimed at excluding fringe parties. Paradoxically, in Britain the bipolarity seems to be weakening most, although voting-procedures in that country are necessarily best suited to a bipolar system.

The specific electoral system employed has considerable consequences for shaping the party system. Admittedly, it would be wrong to generalise. Proportional systems do not necessarily lead to party fragmentation; majority systems do not always have a modifying effect. Austria is an archetype of the former and Britain of the latter. Even in countries which have a majority system, there are usually more than two parties in parliament (in Canada, for example, the majority system has quite different consequences from in Britain) and in numerous countries which practise proportional representation a system has developed which is more or less bipolar. Duverger's famous 'laws' (see above, p. 51) regarding the connection between a particular

61

form of electoral system and a particular type of party system can be at best only a rough guideline, if indeed they serve any useful function at all.[25]

A democracy's workability, liberality and stability, and actually its very existence, depend on a number of factors. The election process does not play the decisive role and is certainly not of overriding importance. Nevertheless, the problems and effects of the electoral system cannot be trivialised or even ignored. Hence, whilst it is pointless to concentrate exclusively on the consequences of the electoral system for the party system, it needs to be noted that voting-regulations can influence other areas, such as political culture and the mechanisms for controlling conflict. Despite highly differing assessments of the problem, there is at least a broad consensus in research that 'there is no single factor connecting the electoral system to the party system'.[26] The electoral system is a type of 'palliative' – as a rule it cannot reorganise a party system, so the idea that it is the 'salvation of democracy' (Ortega y Gasset) bears little relation to reality. But Seymour M. Lipset and Stein Rokkan's broadly accepted and in some respects opposing theory that the party systems in European countries developed because of 'cleavages' (for example, centre/periphery, state/church, town/country, work/capital) and have now become 'frozen'[27] must likewise be relativised in many respects. For example, the significance of the old cleavages may change, and one or two new ones, such as the ecological/economical dimension, have formed.

The electoral process in West Germany is exposed to less criticism than its British and French counterparts. Indeed, it is frequently cited as a model of its kind. Is this really primarily because of its electoral system? Is it not rather the case that some

25. For a very self-critical view on this debate see Maurice Duverger, 'Duverger's Law: Forty Years Later', in Bernard Grofman and Arend Lijphart (eds), *Choosing an Electoral System: Issues and Alternatives*, New York, 1984, pp. 69–84; William H. Riker, 'Duverger's Law Revisited' and 'The Influence of Electoral Systems: Faulty Laws or Faulty Method?', ibid., pp. 19–42 and pp. 43–68. See also Nohlen, *Wahlrecht und Parteiensystem*, pp. 201–20.

26. Klaus von Beyme, *Parteien in westlichen Demokratien*, Munich, 1982, p. 317.

27. Cf. Seymour M. Lipset and Stein Rokkan, 'Cleavages, Structures, Party Systems and Voter Alignments: An Introduction', in Lipset and Rokkan (eds), *Party Systems and Voter Alignments: Cross-National Perspectives*, New York, 1967, pp. 1–66.

foreign observers are fascinated by the 'German model' and therefore tend to consider institutional rules such as voting-rights an important factor in the political system's stability? Here we need to point out a misunderstanding.

Despite numerous proposals for reform, the leeway for effective change is limited. Britain is an example of the way in which the relative-majority system is retained regardless of any criticism. France must serve as an example of the exact opposite (albeit an exceptional case): changes to the electoral system are part of everyday life. Most electoral reforms in Western democracies are limited either to increasing or reducing the degree of proportionality. In this, the restrictive clause practised in West Germany has not been without some effect. In the European Parliament elections, France (5%) and the Netherlands (4%) adopted a restrictive clause.

> Historical reality is characterised by limited choice. Reform debates on the subject of majority system versus proportional representation are of a purely academic nature. This observation is particularly aimed at those academics who maintain this debate and link it to a socio-technological creed.[28]

Although Dieter Nohlen is right in his diagnosis of the limited freedom of option, his conclusions are problematic, because, if political science is to be normatively oriented, it also has an obligation to discuss such theories, even if their realisation is very distant or even seems to be postponed *ad calendas graecas*. The decisive factor is not the question of how relevant a certain suggestion is to practice, but its plausibility. Political science must not be the slave of politics. Hence the following chapter is also concerned with the question of the appropriate electoral system for West Germany, even though the subject is not on the political agenda, either now or in the foreseeable future.

---

28. Nohlen, *Wahlrecht und Parteiensysteme*, p. 199.

4
Voting and Elections in West Germany

Voting-Structure

Typology of Electoral Systems

With regard to the classification of electoral systems, one must distinguish between two separate principles: the *principle of representation*, which relates to the entire electorate, and the *principle of distribution*, which is confined to the individual constituency. This distinction has long been neglected.[1] In a majority system, the purpose of the principle of representation is the formation of a majority by means of an 'amplifying-effect' (whereby the major parties win a greater share of seats than of votes). In proportional representation, on the other hand, the principle of representation aims to achieve a correlation between share of votes and share of seats. Hence the actual technical principle of distribution is less decisive. The principle of distribution is concerned with how the seats are allocated at constituency level but says nothing about the final result. Whilst the principle of representation can combine elements of both majority and proportional representation systems, with the principle of distribution only one or the other is possible.

Hence electoral systems should be classified according to their effects, whilst classification according to the principle of distribution is purely formal. As mentioned above, it does allow a clear distinction between majority and proportional representation systems.[2] The formation of a majority can be achieved in

1. Dieter Nohlen should be commended for having drawn attention to these problems and thereby promoting research into electoral systems. See Dieter Nohlen, 'Begriffliche Einführung', in Dolf Sternberger and Bernhard Vogel (eds), *Die Wahl der Parlamente und anderer Staatsorgane. Ein Handbuch*, vol. 1: *Europa*, Berlin, 1969, pp. 1–54.
2. This caused Eberhard Schütt to classify electoral systems according to the principle of distribution. See Eberhard Schütt, *Wahlsystemdiskussion und par-*

various different ways. If in a given constituency three seats are to be allocated, we are dealing with a type of majority system (because of the enormous advantage given to large parties), even if allocation of the three seats is determined by proportional representation.

The most common type of majority system – whether relative majority or absolute majority – is based on the single-seat constituency. The electoral territory is divided into as many constituencies as there are seats. In the *relative-majority system* the candidate who wins the largest number of votes in the constituency is elected. For an *absolute majority*, a second ballot must take place in those constituencies where no candidate has achieved an overall majority on the first ballot. Either only the two most successful candidates from the first ballot may participate (*pure absolute majority*); or else several candidates may participate, so that victory may then be secured with only a relative majority (*Romanesque majority system*). In a system of proportional representation, constituencies are not essential in theory, but do exist in practice.

The principle of representation in an electoral system does not necessarily have to conform strictly to that of either a majority or a proportional representation system. For example, if an electoral territory consists only of six-seat constituencies, this means that in every constituency seats are allocated according to the principle of proportionality. The principle of representation of this electoral system is approximately halfway between the principle of representation of the majority system and that of proportional representation. An electoral system which makes parliamentary representation of a party dependent upon its gaining 10% of the votes would also be somewhere between the majority system and proportional representation. Furthermore, electoral systems are conceivable in which one half of the MPs are elected according to the principle of proportionality and the other half according to the majority principle. It may appear that this type of electoral system exists in West Germany, but, as there is an adjustment between candidates who are directly elected and

lamentarische Demokratie. Untersuchung grundlegender Aspekte der Alternative Verhältniswahl/Mehrheitswahl, Hamburg, 1973, pp. 35–42.

those who are chosen from the Land lists, the net result is proportional representation.

There is a further complication: an electoral system may produce effects which its theoretical assumptions would not have led one to expect. If, for example, in a three-seat constituency the three main parties achieve roughly the same results, the principle of distribution will be that of proportional representation, the theoretical effects will be those of a majority system, and the practical effects will again be those of proportional representation. This example, albeit hypothetical, shows that the question is not one merely of terminology. The question of labelling is only a superficial problem. Whether or not an electoral system fulfils certain criteria is far more decisive. This catalogue of criteria, which, quite apart from the varying significance of the criteria, must necessarily have very variable results, must apply equally to all electoral systems.[3]

The Federal Constitutional Court, on the other hand, is of a quite different opinion. The classification of electoral systems plays a special role in West Germany, inasmuch as the courts, in their role as administrators of justice,[4] use different criteria as a basis for testing the constitutionality of an electoral system, according to whether it is a majority or proportional representation system. Basically, proportional representation requires equal *success* values, whilst a majority system only requires equal *numerical* values. If by 'numerical value' one means that every vote has the same weighting when the votes are being counted, then 'success value' implies that every vote has fundamentally the same value when allocating seats. Violations of the principle of equal success values are only possible in exceptional cases and to a limited extent (for instance, the 5% hurdle). Hence electoral systems are judged according to different criteria. If the legislature has decided on a certain type of electoral

3. The author has developed a catalogue of criteria and examined various proposed electoral systems in West Germany with this in mind. See Eckhard Jesse, *Wahlrecht zwischen Kontinuität und Reform. Eine Analyse der Wahlsystemdiskussion und der Wahlrechtsänderungen in der Bundesrepublik Deutschland 1949–1983*, Düsseldorf, 1985, pp. 45–50 and 158–210.

4. This is true of the first federal decision regarding voting. See *Entscheidungen des Bundesverfassungsgerichts* (Federal Constitutional Law), 1:208–61. For details see Jochen Abr. Frowein, 'Die Rechtsprechung des Bundesverfassungsgerichts zum Wahlrecht', *Archiv des öffentlichen Rechts*, 99/1974, pp. 72–110.

system, it must always follow it faithfully and consistently. However, the Federal Constitutional Court's dogmatic interpretation of electoral law leads in practice to inconsistencies. This can be seen by considering two examples: first, an example of an election in multi-seat constituencies (natural barrier), and, secondly, an example of a restrictive clause (artificial barrier).

If the election takes place in a four-seat constituency (in 1968 this type of suggestion for reform was under discussion), four seats are allocated according to the proportion of votes received by the parties in the constituencies. If one classifies this four-seat electoral system – according to the principle of distribution – as proportional representation, because the allocation of seats in the constituencies occurs according to the principle of proportionality, then in the eyes of the Federal Constitutional Court it is unconstitutional. If one treats the election process – according to the principle of representation – as a majority system, then the Federal Constitutional Court has no reservations. The result is ridiculous: an electoral system conforms to the constitution if it goes under the name of a majority system because it does not affect numerical-value equality; on the other hand it is deemed unconstitutional if it is considered to be proportional representation, because it contravenes success-value equality. Hence the dilemma centres on problems of terminology.

The same is true of the restrictive-clause ruling: a restrictive clause of more than 5% would probably be considered intolerable by the Federal Constitutional Court, even though it would have no objections to the relative-majority system, which is far more drastic. In its first judgement on voting it laid down the following: 'There must be quite specific, essential reasons to justify the quorum being raised above the standard German level of 5%.'[5] West German electoral research has long made heavy weather of the restrictive-clause condition. Staunch advocates of proportional representation disapprove of it anyway; supporters of the majority system, such as Sternberger, likewise find it unacceptable because it endangers equality of voting. Mainly it was seen as a sort of stop-gap measure. However, the fact that it represents a quite legitimate barrier for departing from pure proportional representation without introducing a

5. *Entscheidungen des Bundesverfassungsgerichts*, 1:256.

majority system has long been ignored. Even today, academics are still expressing criticism, motivated of course by various factors.[6] How can one explain this dogmatism regarding voting? There are two main factors involved. On the one hand serious significance is attributed to the distinction between a restriction which is 'against the system' (artificial) and one which is 'inherent in the system' (natural). This is totally incorrect, because the artificial barrier is no more arbitrary than the natural barrier. Hence the cause of the restrictive effect is of no importance whatsoever, because it is in any case based on practical considerations. Moreover, it is inappropriate to derive the analogous principle of representation from the principle of distribution. The principles of distribution and representation do not necessarily coincide. The legislator can declare his support for the principle of representation of the majority system and try to realise this by setting the restrictive clause at an appropriately high level.

On the other hand, the argument that there are two contrary principles of representation is not conclusive. Dieter Nohlen considers that there are two concepts of representation which oppose one another – the concept of the majority, or, rather, of forming a majority, and the concept of proportional representation. It is true that such a distinction has been maintained in the history of social and political thought, but what is to stop one declaring one's support for a concept of representation which does not make the two extremes absolute? Hans Meyer argues that we should see the two systems as belonging to a continuum. Proportional representation and the majority system are not wholly distinct, he claims, but are 'merely the two extremes of a more or less continuous array of electoral systems which in their different technical forms are distinguished by increasing restrictions towards the smaller parties in favour of the larger parties'.[7] As far as the effect is concerned, this theory

6. See Ulrich Wenner, *Sperrklauseln im Wahlrecht der Bundesrepublik Deutschland*, Bern, 1985. In his study the author claims that the 5% clause is anti-constitutional. In 1986, Dolf Sternberger said that 'the state has to live with this lack of legitimacy as if it were an inherent blemish on the body of the constitution' – *Grund und Abgrund der Macht. Über Legitimität von Regierungen*, new edn with 15 chs, Frankfurt/Main, 1986, p. 345.

7. Hans Meyer, *Wahlsystem und Verfassungsordnung. Bedeutung und Grenzen wahlsystematischer Gestaltung nach dem Grundgesetz*, Frankfurt/Main, 1973, p. 191;

is correct if one disregards the fact that under the British relative-majority system, for example, the original intention was simply to provide a representative for each constituency. However, Meyer overshoots the mark when he makes the principle of the equality of voting-rights absolute and rejects systems which conform strictly to proportional representation. Furthermore, he completely neglects the specific form in which the principle of distribution is expressed. The *cubic electoral system*, for example, which is outlined below, is an example of an artificial product which cannot really be recommended, regardless of its effect.

Therefore, electoral systems must be judged according to the same criteria, regardless of whether one classifies them as proportional representation, majority systems or mixed systems. One can conceive of a whole range of different ways of organising electoral systems. A connection between the principle of distribution, which is based on proportionality, and the principle of representation, which is based on the majority principle, is by no means excluded.

Hence I cannot agree with Dieter Nohlen, who has advocated the following theory based on his concept of two distinct principles of representation: 'Electoral systems should be evaluated primarily according to the extent to which they do justice to the principle of representation given to them and not according to whether they fulfil the functions of the competing principle of representation.'[8] Apart from the fact that, in practice, these two principles cannot be completely distinguished, an adequate evaluation would be impossible if a majority system was examined solely according to whether it creates majorities capable of government, whilst a proportional representation system was examined solely according to whether it guarantees all parties a proportion of seats which corresponds to their proportion of votes. One would arrive at the banal conclusion that in proportional representation a 2% hurdle is better than a 5% hurdle.

Meyer, 'Demokratische Wahl und Wahlsystem', in Josef Isensee and Paul Kirchhof (eds), *Handbuch des Staatsrechts der Bundesrepublik Deutschland*, vol. 2, Heidelberg, 1987, p. 261.

8. Dieter Nohlen, 'Wahlen', in Klaus von Beyme, Ernst-Otto Czempiel, Peter Graf Kielmansegg and Peter Schmoock (eds), *Politikwissenschaft. Eine Grundlegung*, vol. 2: *Der demokratische Verfassungsstaat*, Stuttgart, 1987, p. 97.

Table 4.1 Constituency seats by party membership of those elected
in Bundestag elections, 1949–87

Year	Total	CDU/CSU	SPD	FDP	Others
1949	242	115	96	12	19[a]
1953	242	172	45	14	11[b]
1957	247	194	46	1	6[c]
1961	247	156	91	–	–
1965	248	154	94	–	–
1969	248	121	127	–	–
1972	248	96	152	–	–
1976	248	134	114	–	–
1980	248	121	127	–	–
1983	248	180	68	–	–
1987	248	169	79	–	–

CDU   Christlich Demokratische Union (Christian Democratic Union).
CSU   Christlich-Soziale Union (Christian Social Union).
FDP   Freie Demokratische Partei (Free Democratic Party).
SPD   Sozialdemokratische Partei Deutschlands (Social Democratic Party of
     Germany).
(a) Bayernpartei 11; Deutsche Partei 5; independents 3.
(b) Deutsche Partei 10; Zentrum 1.
(c) Deutsche Partei.
Source: compiled from official statistics.

Eventually the problem would shift to the question of which
was the better principle of representation. It is important that all
electoral systems should be evaluated according to the same
criteria, which must be developed so that they do not have a
built-in bias in favour of a certain process.

Bundestag Voting-Rights

Following the absolute-majority system which was used in the
German Empire and the system of pure proportional representation which existed in the Weimar Republic, the Federal legislature envisaged a system of proportional representation which
would be restricted by provisos only to a very insignificant
extent. In accordance with Article 38 of the Basic Law, MPs are
elected in a universal, direct, free, equal and secret election.
There is no obligation to vote. One is eligible to vote (*active
voting right*) at the age of eighteen. Following a law passed in
1975, the age of majority is now eighteen years and hence there

is also the age at which one may stand for election (*passive voting right*).

In Bundestag elections, 496 seats are allocated (excluding the twenty-two seats in Berlin). Every voter has two votes. With his first vote he votes for the constituency candidates (direct mandate) and with the decisive second vote he votes for a party's regional list of parliamentary candidates. Hence the voter can split his two votes. From the proportion of second votes it is determined how many of the 496 seats each party is entitled to. The total number of seats gained by a party is allocated to its regional lists, after deducting the 248 direct mandates appertaining to the 248 single-seat constituencies. In each constituency, the person with the greatest number of first votes is elected (*relative majority*). The remaining seats are allocated to candidates according to the order on the regional list. Since 1961, all direct mandates have been allocated exclusively to either the candidates of the CDU/CSU or the SPD (see Table 4.1). In earlier elections, a few direct mandates were obtained by the minor parties, but mainly by means of election pacts with the larger parties.

As the above description shows, the electoral system in West Germany is not – contrary to widespread opinion – a 'mixed system' but proportional representation. It is only a mixed system inasmuch as half the MPs are elected directly and half by means of the list. The second vote is decisive for the allocation of seats in the German Bundestag. The principle of proportional voting is limited only by the 5% *hurdle* and by possible *overhang seats* (i.e. constituency seats in excess of the total number of seats to which a party is entitled by its share of second votes).

Parties which achieve less than 5% of the votes or which do not achieve at least three direct mandates (*alternative clause*) cannot participate in the allocation of seats. The votes received by such parties go by the board and hence indirectly benefit parties who have overcome the percentage hurdle. The 5% clause, approved by the Federal Constitutional Court, is intended to ensure the ability of parliament to function properly and to prevent fragmentation of the party system; minority parties such as the Südschleswigsche Wählerverband (South Schleswig Voters' Union, SSW), which stands in the Schleswig-Holstein Landtag (provincial parliament) elections, are excluded by this rule.

Overhang seats can occur if a party achieves more constituency seats in a Land than it is entitled to by its proportion of second votes. These direct mandates are not lost by the party, but in practice they are very rare: to date there have been seventeen of them (and since the Bundestag elections in 1965, when the size of the constituencies was standardised, there have only been four). Compensatory seats for the other parties are not envisaged.

The selection of candidates occurs according to two different processes. Constituency candidates are elected by delegates' conferences in that constituency. The candidates for the Land lists are selected by a secret ballot at Land delegates' conferences. The primary function of the Land list is to give safe seats to the constituency candidates; it is less concerned with 'party planning', if at all. Once the process of selecting candidates is complete, a large number of MPs have in effect already been selected, owing to largely predictable voting-behaviour.

Landtag and local government elections are likewise conducted according to the principles of proportional representation (including the 5% clause), with certain variations in the case of Bavaria and Baden-Württemberg, mainly owing to the increased emphasis on personal elements. In local government elections in these Länder, the voter has the opportunity of accumulating or splitting his vote. To *accumulate*, the voter 'piles up' several votes on one candidate; to *split*, he takes the lists of the individual parties into consideration. Almost everywhere, overhang seats are neutralised by compensatory seats for other parties.

Controversies Surrounding Electoral Systems

Political controversies   Various attempts at reform stand in noteworthy contrast to the constancy of the electoral system in the Federal Republic of Germany.[9] They have nevertheless re-

9. For the period up to 1956 see Erhard H. M. Lange, *Wahlrecht und Innenpolitik. Entstehungsgeschichte und Analyse der Wahlgesetzgebung und Wahlrechtsdiskussion im westlichen Nachkriegs deutschland 1945–1956*, Meisenheim/Glan, 1975. For information on the debate surrounding electoral reform at the time of the 'Grand Coalition', see Rüdiger Bredthauer, *Das Wahlsystem als Objekt von Politik und Wissenschaft. Die Wahlsystemdiskussion in der BRD 1967/68 als politische und wissenschaftliche Auseinandersetzung*, Meisenheim/Glan, 1973. For the ensuing period see Jesse, *Wahlrecht zwischen Kontinuität und Reform*, pp. 129–38.

mained unsuccessful. The Parlamentarischer Rat (Parliamentary Council, an assembly consisting of sixty-five delegates from the Land parliaments), which in 1948–9 drew up the Basic Law and which has been intensively involved in voting-rights, rejected suggestions of anchoring the electoral system in the constitution, with the argument that this would make possible future changes to the system too difficult. The CDU/CSU members of the Parlamentarischer Rat, who wanted to introduce a relative-majority system, were unable to gain the support of the SPD and the smaller parties. Hence this electoral law was only valid for one legislative term, as was the next one. The 1953 attempt by the CDU/CSU-led coalition to introduce a type of 'mixed system' (the 'Lehr Bill') failed mainly because of the hostility of public opinion. The project initiated by the CDU/CSU and the Deutsche Partei (German Party, DP) in 1956, whereby one half of the MPs was to be elected by means of a system of relative majority and the other by proportional representation, likewise caused problems. It was one of the reasons why the FDP left the coalition. The new electoral law had a definitive character and its major points are still valid today.

Following the *Spiegel* affair in 1962, the CDU/CSU and the SPD held tentative, informal talks aimed at forming a Grand Coalition and introducing a majority electoral system. The electoral system remained unchanged, but at the end of 1966 the question arose again. Kurt-Georg Kiesinger, in his inaugural speech as leader of the Grand Coalition, predicted the introduction of such a system, hence automatically implying a two-party system. However, the plan failed because of resistance from certain sectors of public opinion, the FDP and above all the SPD, who, on the one hand, were scared of becoming the 'eternal losers' and, on the other, were loth to alienate their possible coalition partner, the FDP. The most recent debate about changing the electoral system occurred in 1967–8 – at the time it was one of the main topics on the home front – and was both intensive and heated. In March 1968 Paul Lücke, the Federal Minister for the Interior, resigned from office because in the same month the SPD had postponed the subject of 'electoral reform' at their party conference in Nuremberg. The ensuing debate regarding the introduction of three- or four-seat constituencies no longer had any influence over political practice.

Since then the subject has lost all topicality, and political circles no longer consider the possibility of a change in the electoral system. Following the split in the SDP–FDP coalition in 1982, attempts to revive the debate failed. This was also the case in the aftermath of various Landtag elections, where formation of a government was temporarily rendered impossible by the behaviour of the Greens (so-called 'Hamburg' or 'Hesse' situations). Certain sectors of this party saw themselves and still see themselves as an 'anti-party party' (Petra Kelly). The current system of proportional representation remains undisputed.

If one compares the attitudes of the parties on the question of voting-rights, the CDU/CSU parties failed to capitalise on their favourable starting-position and missed their opportunity to introduce a system which was at least partially a majority system, either because they were too brash or too hesitant. Perhaps this has something to do with the fact that the staunchest advocates of the majority system came from different camps: on the one hand from the CSU, with its Bavarian strongholds and its pronounced animosity towards liberalism; on the other, from the 'workers' section' of the CDU, which regarded the FDP as a hindrance to social progress. The attitude of the CDU/CSU can best be described as rhetorical electoral dogmatism in favour of a majority system.

The SPD, which used doggedly to support proportional representation on ideological grounds regardless of the best interests of the electorate, later relaxed its attitude, owing to the party's perpetual lack of success and of its abandonment of mechanical belief in the equality concept. At the time of the Grand Coalition, the SPD's 'stalling-policy',[10] particularly as managed by Herbert Wehner, was very effective. It managed to ensure that the party would in any case be part of the government after 1969, regardless of the election outcome (except in the event of a CDU/CSU absolute majority). It took a flexible position in favour of proportional representation.

The FDP's preference for proportional representation was by no means clear from the outset, because of its tendency to favour, in its own affairs, the electoral system that would pro-

10. Accurately described in Lutz Franke, 'Sozialdemokraten und Wahlreform', *Der Wähler*, n.s., 22/1969, p. 18.

duce the best leadership to suit its needs. However, all other considerations were soon overshadowed by existential interests. In the electoral laws of 1949, 1953 and 1956 the FDP's influence 'tipped the balance': indeed, the party's 'decisive, majority-forming role'[11] is often underestimated. Later it was spared the need to participate in electoral reforms, thanks to shrewd tactics and fortunate constellations. One must credit the FDP with a robust, successful awareness of its own interests.

The role of the small parties is worth only a brief mention. The Deutsche Partei did not vote in favour of any of the three electoral laws. It supported the absolute-majority system, which, it believed, required the voter to vote for a personality rather than a party. This party, which had specific strongholds, had particularly high hopes for the absolute-majority system, especially as it could hope for CDU/CSU support in the second ballot in several constituencies.

It is self-evident that the Kommunistische Partei Deutschlands (Communist Party of Germany, KPD) and Deutsche Kommunistische Partei (German Communist Party, DKP) have unreservedly supported pure proportional representation. In this, their ideological standpoint (orientation towards equality concepts) was just as important as the way the seats are allocated. Ideological conviction converged with their desire to keep their heads above water. Likewise, the National-Demokratische Partei Deutschlands (National Democratic Party of Germany, NPD) was and still is a sharp opponent of majority electoral systems, although it does not advocate pure proportional representation as dogmatically as the extreme left-wing – for example, the NPD's party manifesto does not state any comparative preference. In the case of other smaller parties, it is entirely self-evident that they support proportional representation because of their limited power. They have no influence over the structure of parliamentary voting in any case.

Hence interest constellations inevitably determined the course of debates whenever the opportunity for change arose. Of course, while defending their own interests, the parties had

---

11. Arnulf Baring, in collaboration with Manfred Görtemaker, *Machtwechsel. Die Ära Brandt–Scheel*, Stuttgart, 1982, p. 15.

no compunction about branding their opponents' interests as 'egotistical'.

Academic controversies   Even in the academic world, a topic which was fiercely debated until 1969 is now largely forgotten. The supporters of majority electoral systems suggested numerous variations on the theme – from the relative-majority system with and without a supplementary list to a system with three- or four-seat constituencies. Suggestions with unusual names such as the 'harmonising majority system' and strange methods of counting and weighing votes such as the 'cubic electoral system' likewise figured in their arguments.[12]

Under the former system, a party would receive an additional seat from the list for every MP who was elected according to the principle of relative majority. The list seats would be allocated ('harmonised') in relation to the party's share of votes in the Land, regardless of the number of direct seats won. This precaution was intended to prevent an 'urbanisation' of the SPD and a 'ruralisation' of the CDU/CSU. The idea originally came from Helmut Unkelbach, who formulated it in the 1950s and revived it during the debate on electoral reform in 1967–8. It was taken up and systematised by Joachim Wiesner, who, like Unkelbach, came from the ranks of the 'Cologne School'.

In a 'cubic electoral system', the number of votes received by each party is cubed and seats are allocated in proportion to the result. This suggestion, which came from Helmut Unkelbach and Ferdinand A. Hermens,[13] guaranteed that the party with the most votes would obtain the most seats, ensured it a clear advantage and also prevented the manipulation of constituencies. At the end of the 1960s the distribution of the main parties' strongholds was such that, under a relative-majority system, it was possible for the CDU/CSU to obtain a narrow majority of votes while the SPD obtained a majority of seats. Hermens and Unkelbach's proposal was suggested by the observation that, under majority systems, the number of seats won by a party corresponded approximately to its share of the

12. See for details Jesse, *Wahlrecht zwischen Kontinuität und Reform*, pp. 158–210.
13. See Ferdinand A. Hermens and Helmut Unkelbach, 'Die Wissenschaft und das Wahlrecht', *Politische Vierteljahresschrift*, 8/1967, pp. 2–22.

vote after cubing the number of votes cast for each party ('cubic rule'). Of course, this comical suggestion, which carried functionality to the extreme, was often met with both rejection and astonishment, even amongst supporters of the relative-majority system such as Dolf Sternberger, who considered the whole idea insane.

All these suggestions have the inherent aim of facilitating working majorities, increasing the legitimacy of those in power, promoting the stability of the political system, and at the same time of increasing opportunities for a change in the governing party. In the current party system, the third party absorbs the losses of the main party in power. Under a majority system, it was argued, coalition squabbles would be abandoned, and the major parties would be forced to take a moderate path. Moreover, the majority system would prevent a possible radicalisation of the voters.

The supporters of majority electoral systems were not united. Whilst the 'Cologne School', led by Ferdinand A. Hermens, was more concerned with functional aspects, the 'Heidelberg School', led by Dolf Sternberger, was more concerned with reform itself, whilst ignoring political objections. It is difficult to determine which side was in fact doing more to damage its own interests: the one which juggled with different election processes within the majority-system framework in its attempts to refute any objections from the politicians; or the side which clung to the relative-majority system as the only 'problem-free solution'. Even if the academic supporters of the majority system had 'stuck together', the results would probably not have been fruitful in view of the complicated nexus of interests.

The counter-arguments were varied. Either it was pointed out that some of the consequences of proportional representation predicted by the supporters of the majority system had not manifested themselves at all (such as a radicalisation of the parties, fragmentation of the party system, coalition disputes), or it was argued that the openness of the political order is not ensured by two parties alone. Innovative forces would have to be active at an extra-parliamentary level.

Academic disputes were not always conducted at a high level. Little use was made of empirical electoral research, and many academics and institutes saw themselves as the instruments of their own particular party. The person commissioning the study prejudiced the result. In this sense, the hectic discussions regarding electoral systems at the end of the 1960s did not contribute anything new academically, and the academic debate was eclipsed by the political one.

Since then, there has been little discussion of electoral systems in the West German context. Recently, Günther Willms even spoke of a 'German taboo' on the subject,[14] which is not strictly true inasmuch as there is no real question of sanctions. But it does indeed seem strange that the question of changing the electoral system is rarely mentioned now.[15]

If one weighs up the arguments for and against a majority system in West Germany, the demand for such a system is still by no means completely inappropriate. It would restrict the tendency towards consensus democracy (more or less all-party government), which is in any case overstretched, and would weaken the prevailing tendency for responsibilities to become blurred. The main governing party would no longer be able to justify its behaviour with real or feigned consideration for the smaller coalition partner. After all, in the current party system a change is only possible in certain circumstances; if it does occur it is less because of the electorate than because of the vote of a small party, which admittedly reacts indirectly to changes in voter preferences.

However, three arguments decisively oppose a change in the electoral system. First, reform proposals would be seen as hostile to the small parties, which have fared reasonably well under the existing electoral system. The fact that the system has existed for so long has in itself created a degree of legitimacy which should not be destroyed. Secondly, the fears expressed in the 1950s and even in the 1960s that the Federal Republic would

14. See Günther Willms, 'Ein deutsches Tabu', *Zeitschrift für Politik*, 33/1986, pp. 188–98. For one of the few 'reforms' see Eberhard Schütt-Wetschky, 'Wahlsystem und politisches System in der parlamentarischen Demokratie', *Politische Bildung*, 19.2/1986, pp. 3–17, and 'Verhältniswahl und Mehrheitsregierungen. Unter besonderer Berücksichtigung Großbritanniens, Dänemark und der Bundesrepublik Deutschland', *Zeitschrift für Parlamentsfragen*, 18/1987, pp. 94–109.

15. See Eckhard Jesse, 'Soll das Wahlsystem geändert werden? Überlegungen zu einem nicht aktuellen Thema', in Rupert Breitling and Winand Gellner (eds), *Politische Studien. Zum 65. Geburtstag von Erwin Faul*, Gerlingen, 1988, vol. 2, pp. 27–41.

prove to be a 'fair-weather democracy' requiring institutional support (Ferdinand A. Hermens) have long lost their force. West Germany has become a liberal democracy with an established political culture which manages to control diverging interests without a majority system. There is no sign of a radicalisation of voting-behaviour. Thirdly, proportional representation has in many respects produced the same effects as are generally ascribed to majority systems: the party system is basically bipolar, with a government and an opposition; the voter knows before an election who is going to form a coalition with whom and hence more or less decides on the government; an increase in ideology or even radicalism amongst the parties has failed to materialise; and coalition quarrels are very rare. The following paradox remains: proportional representation has been preserved because many of the demands made by supporters of the majority system have been fulfilled, in spite of the fact that the current electoral system is based on proportional representation.

Changes in Voting-Rights

Whilst the principle of proportional representation has remained intact since 1949, there have nevertheless been a series of changes in voting rights which have influenced the outcome of elections to a certain extent and which hence must not be underestimated. The most important changes are listed in Table 4.2.

The 5% *hurdle* was added to the electoral law by the minister–presidents of the Länder in 1949. Whilst in 1949 it only applied at Land level, since 1953 a party has had to achieve at least 5% of the votes in West Germany as a whole in order to participate in the allocation of seats in the Bundestag. An exception was made (in a clause introduced in 1953) where the party gained one direct mandate (increased to three in 1956). The restrictive clause accelerated party concentration but did not cause it. The percentage hurdle is not so high as to give the impression that founding a party is pointless, but at the same time is high enough to make it difficult for fringe parties to exist. Whilst I consider the 5% hurdle to be not only legitimate in principle but also necessary, other objections may be raised, which admit-

Table 4.2 Changes in voting-rights in the Federal Republic since 1949

Type of change	Year	Effect	Evaluation	Significance
Introduction and tightening of the 5% clause	1949 1953 1956	Strengthened the larger parties, weakened the smaller parties	Positive (some reservations)	High
Introduction of the second vote	1953	Strengthened the FDP	Negative	High
Introduction of the postal vote	1956	Increased the size of the electorate; benefited the 'middle-class' parties	Positive	Medium
Lowering of the age of majority from 21 to 18	1970	Increased the size of the electorate; strengthened the 'Greens': weakened the CDU/CSU	Positive (some reservations)	High
Introduction of the vote for German expatriates	1985	Increased the size of the electorate; gave a minimal advantage to 'middle-class' parties	Positive (some reservations)	Low
Replacement of the d'Hondt 'highest number system' with the Hare–Niemeyer system	1985	Reduction of 'overhang' seats; possible strengthening of small parliamentary parties by one seat	Positive	Medium

Source: compiled by the author.

tedly do not question the actual principle of the clause. These are discussed later on.

The *second-vote system* was introduced in 1953. The voter was given the opportunity of using his two votes in different ways (so-called 'splitting'). Incidentally, the first vote has never acquired the character of a 'personality vote', because the voters do not make their decision on basis of the personality of the constituency candidate. Nevertheless, 'splitting' is increasingly being used (see Table 4.3). This is mainly because many people use their second vote in favour of the FDP. Electoral research cannot decide whether these are 'true' FDP voters who cast their first vote for the party which is to form a coalition with the FDP, or voters for other parties who 'loan' their second vote to the FDP either because they want to help it over the 5% hurdle or because they believe it to be a compromise if one votes for one party with the first vote and a different party with the second vote. In any case, the second-vote system, which in some conditions can lead to a distortion of the electorate's intentions, is not understood by a considerable part of the electorate.

The *postal vote* results from an amendment made to the law in 1956. It is generally recognised that the postal vote is essential, because in a democracy the right to participate in decision-making must in principle be available to all citizens. However, whether the conditions attached to the postal vote should be made more difficult is a different matter. Since 1976 the number of postal voters has been more than 10%. It is known that postal voters tend to favour 'middle-class' parties, but the Greens have also profited from postal votes.

The *age at which one is eligible to vote* was reduced from twenty-one to eighteen in 1970. The opinion of politicians of all parties, which at the time was regarded as self-evident, that the reform reflected the needs of the moment was understandable given the unrest amongst sectors of the youth population, particularly students, but the reform was by no means urgently necessary from a legal point of view. The change has benefited the SPD in particular, and since 1980 the Greens have also profited from it.

Seat allocation is carried out according to a calculation method based on mathematical proportion which was invented by Hare and Niemeyer, following a change to the system in 1985. This took over from the so-called 'highest-number system' invented

Table 4.3 Extent of 'vote-splitting' in Bundestag elections, 1957–87
(as a percentage of second votes; excluding postal votes)

Year	Same as first vote	Different party	Invalid
1957	91.6	6.4	2.0
1961	93.7	4.3	2.0
1965	91.4	6.5	2.1
1969	90.5	7.8	1.8
1972	90.5	8.8	0.8
1976	93.2	6.0	0.8
1980	89.2	10.1	0.7
1983	88.6	10.9	0.5
1987	85.7	13.7	0.6

Source: compiled from official statistics.

by d'Hondt. In the Hare–Niemeyer method, the seats for the parties are allocated in a single counting-process (in d'Hondt's system, by means of the series of divisors 1, 2, 3, 4, 5, 6, etc.). The allocation of seats is carried out by processing the number of votes cast for a party. In the Hare–Niemeyer system the total votes for a party are multiplied by the number of seats. This product is divided by the total number of votes. The party receives the number of seats before the decimal point. The remaining seats are allocated to parties in order of the largest fractions after the decimal point. The new allocation method overcomes the slight disadvantage experienced by smaller parties. This can bring the FDP and the Greens one additional seat each. Furthermore, the change makes it more difficult for 'overhang' mandates to arise.

Voting-rights for German expatriates were introduced for the 1987 Bundestag elections. Initially all Germans living in the twenty-one member states of the European Council were allowed to vote, as well as other expatriates who had not been away from Germany for more than ten years. In both cases it is a precondition that before moving away the expatriate had spent at least three months in the territory in which the Basic Law operates. In the 1987 Bundestag elections only just over 5% of the 500,000 eligible expatriates made use of their vote, which was fewer than had been expected.

Among suggestions for further changes in voting-rights is the proposal to introduce a *restricted–open list*. In its concluding report in 1976, the committee of inquiry on constitutional reform proposed giving greater powers to the 'party citizen' and the 'election citizen'.[16] With regards to the latter, it was proposed that the voter should be able to use his second vote (as in the voting-system for the Bavarian Landtag) to change the order of candidates on the party list. The list is 'restricted–open' because, while the voter can change the order of candidates, he cannot change any of the names on the list, but is bound by the parties' pre-selection. Whereas to date the membership of the Bundestag has been determined by lists whose order is fixed by the parties, this reform proposal would mean that those candidates with the best election results would be elected.

Hence membership of the Bundestag would no longer be largely predetermined. In such a system, the citizen would have greater participatory rights and the legitimacy of those elected would be reinforced. Admittedly, there is a danger of setting one's expectations too high. It would depend very much on whether an 'element of personality voting'[17] could in fact be adequately developed in Bundestag elections. In this regard, the criticism sometimes levelled at the 'rigid list' overshoots the mark when it emphasises that the voter can *only* choose whether or not to vote for a Land list; if he votes for it, he accepts the order of candidates determined by the parties. The little word 'only' suggests that the voter is deprived of power and overemphasises the personality element. In fact, however, the party vote is incomparably more significant than candidate preference. To date, politicians have not taken up this suggestion for increasing participation.

Some suggestions by politicians or academics, or with support from public opinion, are neither worth mentioning nor relevant to practice. This is true of the proposal to grant local government voting-rights to foreigners living in Germany (instead, naturalisation should be made easier) and of proposals to make it easier for women to be elected (for example, by establishing double

16. Cf. Presse- und Informationszentrum des Deutschen Bundestags, *Beratungen und Empfehlungen zur Verfassungsreform. Schlußbericht der Enquête-Kommission Verfassungsreform des Deutschen Bundestags*, pt 1, Bonn, 1976, esp. pp. 55–70.

17. Joachim Henkel, *Die Auswahl der Parlamentsbewerber*, Berlin, 1976, p. 76.

constituencies). Other reforms, however, are desirable, although they currently have no prospect of being realised. This is true of proposals to abolish 'overhang' seats and to abolish the 'alternative clause'. The 'overhang' seats which arise are not due to the effects which the electoral system has on individuals but are the result of many different causes (such as the way the constituencies are divided; in the past the d'Hondt system was also a factor, because this disadvantages small Länder owing to the 'greatest average' principle). The so-called 'alternative clause,' which is currently meaningless (unlike in the elections of 1953 and 1957) is open to manipulation and undermines the restrictive clause. A small party which has considerable local strongholds should not be considered 'more worthy of representation' than a party whose votes are distributed throughout the whole country, quite apart from the fact that one can avoid the 5% clause by gaining three direct mandates in, for example, Bremen, Hessen and Bavaria.

The most useful change that can be envisaged would involve a modification of two proposals mentioned above. First, the second-vote system would have to be completely abolished. Hence, a single vote would benefit the constituency candidate just as much as the party. Reverting to the past (in 1949 elections took place according to this method) would be a step into the future. The drawbacks mentioned could be eliminated in this way, and even the personal element could be brought into play, to a certain extent at least. People might become more likely to vote for a candidate whose party they did not support. Admittedly this factor would not be particularly significant.

This reform would need to be introduced in conjunction with a second one: as votes for parties who do not achieve 5% are completely wasted, the electorate should be granted a contingency vote. This would be valid, if required, unless it too has been given to a party which wins less than 5% of the vote. The effect of the 5% clause would not be undermined, but many of its side-effects would: many voters do not vote for a small party simply because they fear that their vote will be wasted. Likewise, the reverse may also apply: supporters of a large party may vote for a small party in order to help it over the 5% hurdle so that it can participate in a planned coalition. This alternative vote is nothing unusual. In Australia it is practised under the conditions of absolute majority for the purpose of avoiding a second ballot.

Both suggested reforms would improve the current electoral system in terms of participation and efficiency and make it easier to understand.[18] For the time being, political difficulties may prevent the change from being carried out, but, at the request of the FDP, some Länder are already in the process of installing such a system.

Electoral Sociology

Electorate Research

As shown in the previous section, there is no clear distinction between research into voting and research into the electorate. The analysis of election results creates enormous methodological difficulties, although electoral research is highly advanced, thanks to some ingenious instruments. In spite of this, its strength lies in interpreting the results of an election rather than in being able to predict its outcome. We are a long way from a general theory of voting-behaviour, in so far as this is at all possible. Criticism of empirical electoral research even leans towards the belief that, despite considerable effort, the scientific yield is stagnating, or in any case is not automatically increasing in step with the refinement of methods. A basic distinction can be made between the *analysis of individual data* and the *analysis of aggregate data*, although there are of course numerous overlaps and cross-overs.[19]

The analysis of *individual data* is based in particular on evaluation of the results of surveys. The individual voter's decision can be assessed in this way. Particularly informative are so-called 'panels'. This means that the same person is questioned several times; in this way one avoids memory lapses and can recognise both constancy and change in voting-behaviour, even though in some circumstances asking questions several times

18. For a detailed justification see Jesse, *Wahlrecht zwischen Kontinuität und Reform*, pp. 254–60, 307–11, 358–67.
19. For details see for example Werner Kaltefleiter and Peter Nißen, *Empirische Wahlforschung. Eine Einführung in Theorie und Technik*, Paderborn, 1980.

can have a distorting effect. In addition, survey data are necessarily imprecise, even when one considers that the 'rough data'
are processed and weighted accordingly.

Particularly controversial are the so-called 'voter movement
summaries' practised by the infas-Institut to establish the number of floating voters. On the one hand, they reveal something
which has long been neglected – namely, how complicated voter
movement is – because, owing to so-called 'voter exchange',
part of the gross movement does not appear in the net summaries. On the other hand, these voter-movement models must
be seen as unreliable because they are based partly on surveys
and hence can only be approached with care, as the later
comparison with representative statistics shows.[20]

Representative election statistics are likewise based on individual data. Votes are categorised according to sex and age
group in representatively selected constituencies. In this way, it
is possible to obtain precise details regarding electoral participation and voting in relation to sex and age.[21] The disadvantage
is that sex and age do not decisively characterise voting behaviour, or, in any case, not nearly as much as the voter's social
milieu.

The analysis of *aggregate data* takes the actual vote and corre-
lates it with socio-economic characteristics (for instance, the
percentage of those employed in industry). In this way, a
correlation between individual social structure and specific
types of voting-behaviour may be shown. Admittedly, these
correlations suggest a precision which is by no means necessarily true of the individual. The result may be that false con-
clusions are drawn from these correlations. For example, the
data for the 1950s and 1960s show that electoral turn-out in-

20. See for example Claus Laemmerhold, 'Auf Biegen oder Brechen: die
Nichtwähler im Prokrustesbett der Wanderungsbilanzen', and Manfred
Küchler, 'Die Schätzung von Wählerwanderungen: neue Lösungsversuche', in
Max Kaase and Hans-Dieter Klingemann (eds), *Wahlen und politisches System.
Analysen aus Anlaß der Bundestagswahl 1980*, Opladen, 1983, pp. 624–31, 632–51.
For a defence see Fritz Krauß and Menno Smid, 'Wählerwanderungsanalysen.
Ein Vergleich verschiedener Ansätze am Beispiel der Bundestagswahl 1980',
Zeitschrift für Parlamentsfragen, 12/1981, pp. 83–108.

21. Cf. the two studies by Joachim Hofmann-Göttig: *Die jungen Wähler. Zur
Interpretation der Jungwählerdaten der 'Repräsentativen Wahlstatistik' für Bundestag,
Landtage und Europaparlament 1953–1984*, Frankfurt/Main, 1984; *Emanzipation mit
dem Stimmzettel. 70 Jahre Frauenwahlrecht in Deutschland*, Bonn, 1986.

creased as the number of refugees from the East in a given constituency rose. It would be rash to deduce from this that refugees are more enthusiastic about voting than the local inhabitants. It may well be that the high electoral turn-out in those constituencies was also due to the fact that some locals were reacting against the considerable number of refugees. The analysis of aggregate data cannot analyse why the voter votes for an individual party, in the way that the analysis of individual data does.

It is obvious that the methodological instrument influences the result to a certain extent. Approaches which are more *socio-psychologically* oriented and which prefer the survey method of research emphasise individual determining factors of voting-behaviour, whilst more *socio-structurally* oriented approaches emphasise the attachment to social groups. It is known that individuals behave differently according to the environment they are acting in. In this way, electoral research is tending increasingly to combine individual data and aggregate data.

It is neither conceivable nor desirable to abolish opinion research from the life of a democracy; but, at the same time, opinion research is exposed to some severe criticism. The counter-arguments are less concerned with the precision of the results than with the influence that such research has. So far as manipulating results is concerned, this is relatively rare, because no institute can afford to present faked data in the face of stiff competition. Two other criticisms are more important.

First, it is argued that publishing predictions can in some circumstances influence the outcome of an election. For example, it is claimed that the only reason why the FDP managed to enter the Bundestag in the 1983 elections was that, during the campaign, public-opinion research institutes either suggested or actually stated that there had been an increase in the proportion of FDP votes, so that *tactical* voters decided to vote for the FDP because they had reason to believe that their vote would not be wasted.[22] Even if this is true, it is not a valid objection to opinion

22. Cf. Rainer-Olaf Schultze, 'Regierungswechsel bestätigt. Eine Analyse der Bundestagswahl vom 6. März 1983', in Hans-Georg Wehling (ed.), *Westeuropas Parteiensystem im Wandel*, Stuttgart, 1983, p. 68. Schulze has frequently raised objections to public-opinion research; see for example his 'Meinungsforschung: vom aktiven Wähler zum passiven Befragten, in Peter Haungs and Eckhard

research. It is neither desirable nor even possible to ban the publication of election prognoses, for they represent – at least for the interested voter – valuable information on which to base one's vote.

A second argument claims that opinion research weakens, if not undermines, the principle of representative democracy, by regularly informing the electorate of popular preferences. The parties, it is argued, should show leadership qualities and should not always follow the will of the people.[23] This 'public-opinion democracy' (Theodor Eschenburg) does indeed have its drawbacks, but is it really the case that in West Germany political leadership is generally sacrificed on the altar of political show-business? Moreover, it is not necessarily a disadvantage for parties to be aware of the electorate's opinion on various matters.

Public-opinion research is certainly not powerless, but neither is it all-powerful. One of the main reasons for the impressive development of electoral research in West Germany has been the increase in surveys.[24] In spite of this there are incalculables which Friedrich Karl Fromme describes with the expression ' "The voter" – the unknown being'.[25] It is impossible, however highly polished the technique may be, to predict voting-behaviour with precision, especially as voter behaviour is changing more rather than less. (In this sense there are also limits to so-called 'custom-made' electoral laws.) There is a particular paradox in the fact that, on the one hand, the democratic constitutional state takes every all precaution to 'encode'

Jesse(eds), *Parteien in der Krise? In- und ausländische Perspektiven*, Cologne, 1987, pp. 169–74. For the opposite viewpoint see Gebhard Kirchgässner, 'Der Einfluß von Meinungsumfragen auf das Wahlergebnis', in Hans-Dieter Klingemann and Max Kaase (eds), *Wahlen und politischer Prozeß. Analysen aus Anlaß der Bundestagswahl 1983*, Opladen, 1986, pp. 232–47.

23. See Wilhelm Hennis, *Meinungsforschung und repräsentative Demokratie*, Tübingen, 1957.

24. For a summary see Max Kaase, 'Politische Meinungsforschung in der Bundesrepublik Deutschland', *Politische Vierteljahresschrift*, 18/1977, pp. 452–75; Dieter Oberndörfer, 'Politische Meinungsforschung und Politik', in Max Kaase (ed.), *Wählerverhalten in der Bundesrepublik Deutschland. Studien zu ausgewählten Problemen der Wahlforschung aus Anlaß der Bundestagswahl 1976*, Berlin, 1978, pp. 13–18.

25. Friedrich Karl Fromme, 'Der überschaubare Wähler', *Frankfurter Allgemeine Zeitung*, 10 February 1988, p. 1.

the act of voting by means of the secret vote, and that, on the other hand, empirical electoral research then uses costly methods to 'decode' the vote.

Factors that Influence Voting-Behaviour

It is difficult to summarise voting-behaviour in Bundestag elections, because a summary, by its very nature, cannot give adequate coverage to the specific characteristics of and changes in voting-behaviour.[26] The voter clearly perceives a type of bipolar party system. In the 1950s and 1960s there was a 'middle-class majority', against which social democracy was in a structural minority position. In the 1970s the CDU/CSU was in opposition to the SPD-FDP camp, and since 1982 the SPD has once again been in opposition. These particular characteristics can be shown very well with reference to the voting-behaviour of those citizens who voted for the FDP with their second vote. Their first vote – unless it is given to the FDP itself – generally goes to the candidate of the party with which the FDP wishes to form a coalition (see Table 4.4). Between 1953 and 1965, and again in 1983 and 1987, this was the CDU/CSU, and, between 1969 and 1980, the SPD. Hence, these voters did not express any preference for a particular personality with their first vote. Similar characteristics, albeit not quite so extreme, are shown in the first and second votes for the Greens. In the interest of an alternating party system, it would be desirable for them to move closer to the SPD, so that two 'camps' would be in opposition to

26. For a summary of this see for example Rainer-Olaf Schultze, 'Wählerverhalten und Parteiensystem in der Bundesrepublik Deutschland. Konstanz und Wandel in Wählerverhalten und Parteienlandschaft', in Wehling, *Westeuropas Parteiensystem im Wandel*, pp. 9–44; Hans-Dieter Klingemann, 'Der "mündige" Wähler? Ein Ansatz zur Erklärung des Wählerverhaltens, dargestellt am Beispiel der Bundestagswahl 1983', *Politische Bildung*, 19.2/1986, pp. 33–44; Thomas Ellwein and Joachim Jens Hesse, *Das Regierungssystem der Bundesrepublik Deutschland*, 6th edn, Opladen, 1987, esp. pp. 220–33; Forschungsgruppe Wahlen (Manfred Berger *et al.*), 'Die Konsolidierung der Wende. Eine Analyse der Bundestagswahl 1987', *Zeitschrift für Parlamentsfragen*, 18/1987, pp. 253–84; Ursula Feist and Hubert Krieger, 'Alte und neue Scheidelinien des politischen Verhaltens. Eine Analyse zur Bundestagswahl vom 25. Januar 1987', *Aus Politik und Zeitgeschichte*, supplement to *Das Parlament*, B 12/1987, pp. 33–47. Particularly informative is Wilhelm Bürklin, *Wählerverhalten und Wertewandel*, Opladen, 1988.

Table 4.4 Combination of first and second votes for the CDU/CSU, SPD and FDP in Bundestag elections, 1953–87 (as a percentage of second votes; excluding postal votes)

Second votes for	First vote for			First vote for		
	CDU/CSU	SPD	FDP	CDU/CSU	SPD	FDP
	1953			*1957*		
CDU/CSU	87.1	1.1	5.6	93.4	1.0	0.9
SPD	0.7	97.0	0.5	1.3	95.0	0.5
FDP	9.7	1.1	85.3	7.5	3.8	85.0
	1961			*1965*		
CDU/CSU	95.5	1.0	1.1	93.9	2.3	1.4
SPD	1.5	95.5	0.6	2.2	94.7	0.6
FDP	8.1	3.1	86.5	20.9	6.7	70.3
	1969			*1972*		
CDU/CSU	93.4	3.1	1.1	96.8	1.5	0.7
SPD	3.1	93.4	1.4	1.8	94.1	3.0
FDP	10.6	24.8	62.0	7.9	52.9	38.2
	1976			*1980*		
CDU/CSU	97.1	1.1	0.8	96.9	1.3	0.8
SPD	1.2	95.0	2.5	2.1	92.4	3.4
FDP	8.0	26.9	60.7	13.3	35.5	48.5
	1983			*1987*		
CDU/CSU	96.0	2.0	1.0	95.3	1.9	1.3
SPD	1.7	95.2	0.4	1.9	92.7	0.7
FDP	58.3	10.1	29.4	43.2	13.1	38.7

Source: compiled from official statistics.

one another and the SPD would not find itself again in the structural minority position that it occupied during the 1950s and 1960s (in an 'asymmetrical party system').

From time to time, election campaigns are conducted as if they were a matter of life and death. Admittedly, exaggerations and polemics are part of the ritual of election campaigns – moralising indignation is therefore unfounded – but does the polarisation thus aggravated disperse again once the campaign is over? The fact that the election campaign is often superficial may be connected with the parties' awareness that the people's level of political knowledge is not particularly high (compared with the ideal). Electoral researchers have differing opinions on the extent to which election campaigns influence undecided voters, and on whether they primarily serve to mobilise the parties' own supporters. In any case, the electorate's rationality may be only limited, in view of its traditional behaviour and relative immunity to election campaign slogans; and the concept of the 'rational voter' can be ascribed only nominal value as an explanation.[27]

So far as electoral turn-out is concerned, West Germany is at the top of the league of democracies where there is no obligation to vote, and has been since the 1950s. Researchers into political culture consider that this is due less to an increase in the need to participate in political life than to the German tendency to view the act of voting as a common duty. The turn-out rates for women matched those for men in the 1970s. Every election confirms the fact that the young voters have just as little enthusiasm for voting as old voters. The 'non-voters' are not a homogeneous group, although abstaining from voting in West Germany is not primarily an act of protest, or, at least, is not a protest against the political system as a whole so much as a protest against a particular party. As we get further away from the last census, the number of those people eligible to vote who were prevented from voting – who, for example, did not receive a polling-card because they had not informed the authorities that they had moved – is increasing. This factor must also be considered when considering the (relatively low) electoral turn-out of 84.4% in 1987. In view of this, the accuracy of the following statement is questionable:

> The decline in electoral turn-out, not only in Landtag and European elections but now in Bundestag elections as well, most definitely signals increasing scepticism as to whether elections are in fact the
> · most important element of representative/democratic and conventional participation.[28]

27. For details see Hans Rattinger, 'Empirische Wahlforschung auf der Suche nach dem rationalen Wähler', *Zeitschrift für Politik*, 27/1980, pp. 44–58. For a fairly idealistic view see Heiner Flohr, *Parteiprogramme in der Demokratie. Ein Beitrag zur Theorie der rationalen Politik*, Göttingen, 1968, esp. pp. 165–89.

28. See Rainer-Olaf Schultze 'Die Bundestagswahl 1987 – eine Bestätigung des Wandels', *Aus Politik und Zeitgeschichte*, supplement to *Das Parlament*, B 12/1987, p. 9.

This statement is certainly not 'most definite'.

Empirical electoral research focuses on 'floating voters' rather than the loyal party voters and the non-voters.[29] Their proportion can be said to have grown compared with the 1950s, owing to the decrease in party identification (which is still considerable, however). The decline in the proportion of loyal voters is an expression of the greater openness and social mobility of society compared with the 1950s and 1960s, although one cannot deduce from this that West Germany is a 'middle-class society' (Helmut Schelsky), or speak sweepingly of the 'end of ideologies' (Daniel Bell). Changes in the social structure leading to the increasing dissolution of homogeneous environments – the four major social milieus which once characterised Germany (Catholic; conservative; middle-class/Protestant; socialist) disintegrated at the end of the Weimar Republic[30] – have also had some effects on voting-behaviour: in 1950 the electorate consisted of 31.4% self-employed (including members of the family who helped out), 4.2% civil servants, 15.8% white-collar workers and 48.6% blue-collar workers, whilst the figures for 1985 were as follows: 12.9%, 9.4%, 38.3% and 39.4%, respectively. Of course there is no linear correlation between changes in the social statistics and the individual party vote. Floating voters, who are affected by a particularly large number of opposing factors ('cross-pressures'), are not characterised by particular socio-structural characteristics. Owing to the decline in significance of voting for a party for purely traditional reasons, which is to be expected in a society which is not characterised by class barriers, electoral research is now moving towards developing systematic voter typologies according to 'lifestyles', which include, for example, basic orientations (e.g. materialist or post-materialist), attitudes to career and leisure, and religious/philosophical views.[31] These 'lifestyles' partly overlap with traditional lines of conflict.

29. See for example Rainer-Olaf Schultze, 'Wechselwähler', in Dieter Nohlen (ed.), *Pipers Wörterbuch zur Politik*, Munich, 1985, vol. 1, pp. 1133–6.

30. On this subject see M. Rainer Lepsius, 'Parteiensystem und Sozialstruktur: zum Problem der Demokratisierung der deutschen Gesellschaft' (1966), in Gerhard A. Ritter (ed.), *Die deutschen Parteien vor 1918*, Cologne, 1973, pp. 56–80.

31. See Peter Gluchowski, 'Lebensstile und Wandel der Wählerschaft in der Bundesrepublik Deutschland', *Aus Politik und Zeitgeschichte*, supplement to *Das Parlament*, B 12/1987, pp. 18–32.

Whilst in the 1950s and 1960s the *religious* and *welfare-state* lines of conflict were the decisive characteristic of voting-behaviour (with voters committed to the churches or the trade unions rather than simply belonging), in the 1980s an additional area of conflict emerged – the *ecological* dimension. One can ascribe typical occupational groups to certain lifestyles (see Figure 4.1). Strong conflicts of loyalty are unavoidable in this. Opinions within electoral research as to how these three lines of conflict should be weighted[32] are just as diverse as those regarding the degree of internalisation of post-materialist values amongst voters. Are we really dealing with a 'silent revolution' (Ronald Inglehart)? Is it true that 'new politics' is suppressing 'old politics' (Hildebrandt and Dalton)? Any prediction regarding the future development of the Greens is heavily dependent on the answers to these questions.[33]

Despite the process of secularisation and consequent decline in the Catholic milieu in West Germany, it would nevertheless be wrong to neglect or even ignore the role of religion in voting-behaviour, because certain value systems are still being handed down from one generation to the next. As in the 1950s, the CDU/CSU is dominant amongst Catholics.[34]

The question of how significant the economic situation and the personality of the Chancellor (or candidate for the chancellorship) are in voting-behaviour is also disputed. Electoral researchers found the successes of the CDU/CSU in the 1950s due

32. See for example Dieter Oberndörfer, Hans Rattinger and Karl Schmitt, 'Wirtschaftlicher Wandel, religiöser Wandel und Wertwandel: Eine Einführung', in *Wirtschaftlicher Wandel, religiöser Wandel und Wertwandel. Folgen für das politische Verhalten in der Bundesrepublik Deutschland*, Berlin, 1985, pp. 9–41.

33. See for example Wilhelm Bürklin, 'Die Grünen und die "Neue Politik". Abschied vom Dreiparteiensystem', *Politische Vierteljahresschrift*, 22/1981, pp. 359–82; Wilhelm Bürklin, 'Neue Werte - Eine Herausforderung für das poltische System?', in Heinrich Oberreuter (ed.), *Wahrheit statt Mehrheit? An den Grenzen der parlamentarischen Demokratie*, Munich, 1986, pp. 85–103; for more detailed information see Bürklin, *Wählerverhalten und Wertewandel*.

34. See Karl Schmitt, *Konfession und Wahlverhalten in der Bundesrepublik Deutschland*, Berlin, 1990. Cf. this author's preliminary studies: 'Inwieweit bestimmt auch heute noch die Konfession das Wahlverhalten? Konfession, Parteien und politisches Verhalten in der Bundesrepublik', *Der Bürger im Staat*, 34/1984, pp. 95–107; 'Religiöse Bestimmungsfaktoren des Wahlverhaltens. Entkonfessionalisierung mit Verspätung?', in Oberndörfer, Rattinger and Schmitt, *Wirtschaftlicher Wandel*, pp. 291–329: see also, Franz U. Pappi, 'Die konfessionell-religiöse Konfliktlinie in der deutschen Wählerschaft. Entstehung, Stabilität und Wandel', ibid., pp. 263–90.

Figure 4.1 Lines of conflict in West German voting-behaviour

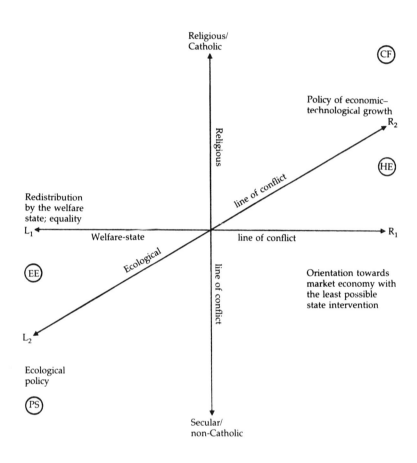

CF   Catholic farmer.
HE   Higher employee in technology within the manufacturing-sector.
EE   Employee in the environmental sector of industry.
PS   Protestant skilled worker.

Source: Rainer-Olaf Schultze, 'Wählerverhalten und Parteiensystem der Bundesrepublik Deutschland. Konstanz und Wandel Wählerverhalten und Parteienlandschaft', in Hans-Georg Wehling (ed.), *Westeuropas Parteiensystem im Wandel*, Stuttgart, 1983, p. 41.

not least to the upturn in the economy (the 'economic miracle') and Adenauer's personality. This so-called 'Chancellor bonus' is said to have been particularly strong in 1972 (when the elections were dubbed 'Brandt elections') and extremely low in 1987, if indeed it existed at all. A statement such as the one made by Werner Kaltefleiter with particular reference to floating voters is somewhat rash, or at least is not based on empirical proof:

> In the long-term average, approximately 50% of the changes be-tween two elections can be explained by the electorate's assessment of the main politicans, measured by the dimensions of how nice they are and their ability to achieve. A further 50% are based on the topics in an election, of which again an average of 50% are covered by ensuring future economic prospects.[35]

This weighting is problematic because it disregards the connec-tion between the degree of improvement or deterioration in economic conditions and voting-behaviour. 'Long-term' average values may hide more information than they impart.

As shown by representative election statistics, the electoral year 1972 in many respects represents a caesura.[36] Since then, the proportions of men and women in the major parties have balanced out; by contrast, in the 1950s and 1960s the CDU/CSU was predominantly a 'women's party' and the SPD a 'men's party'. With regard to age, the trend has been practically the opposite. Whilst in the first elections in West Germany there were hardly any differences between the major parties, the CDU/CSU has increasingly become an 'old' party and the SPD a 'young' party, although recently the SPD has suffered losses amongst the younger generation in particular, owing to the electoral successes of the Greens. Age-specific differences clearly eclipse sex-specific differences. Opinions differ greatly as to whether voting for the Greens is an expression of protest behaviour in a youthful phase of life ('life-cycle theory') or the expression of a change which has occurred within a particular

35. Werner Kaltefleiter, *Vorspiel zum Wechsel. Eine Analyse der Bundestagswahl 1976*, Berlin, 1977, p. 244.
36. See Eckhard Jesse, 'Die Bundestagswahlen von 1972 bis 1987 im Spiegel der repräsentativen Wahlstatistik', *Zeitschrift für Parlamentsfragen*, 18/1987, pp. 232–42.

generation and which is still sustained ('generation theory').[37] The convergence of voting-behaviour is strongly connected with the change in the image of women over the past two decades: female emancipation has notably benefited the SPD.

There is a major difficulty in weighting the individual factors. How important is the so-called 'Chancellor bonus'? How strongly (and, above all, how) does high unemployment influence voting-behaviour? Does the change in social structure have a significant influence on election results? How pronounced is party identification, and how pronounced is religious orientation? Rainer-Olaf Schultze distinguishes between structural and non-structural factors.[38] In the former category he includes, for example, the social structure and the media system as well as superordinate cultural conditions, such as political culture. In the latter category he includes political/situational constellations such as the general climate of public opinion and economic influences, whereby the voter's perception of the economic situation is as important as the actual, 'objective' situation.[39] Structural factors may also change, although admittedly much more slowly than non-structural ones. Examples of this are the – actual or supposed – change in values, which may have more long-term effects on voting-behaviour and has either already led to, or could in the future lead to, a new line of conflict.

Elections at Different Political Levels

Whilst this analysis has so far concentrated almost exclusively on Bundestag elections, this section also examines European, Landtag and local government elections. On average, one election takes place every year for the West German citizen. Whilst Bundestag elections are 'major' elections, other elections are 'minor' elections, which are mainly, although not exclusively, determined by Federal policy. The results sometimes differ, but the rules are the same in principle.

37. For details, see Wilhelm Bürkin, *Grüne Politik. Ideologische Zyklen, Wähler und Parteiensysteme*, Opladen, 1984.

38. Schultze, 'Regierungswechsel bestätigt', in Wehling, *Westeuropas Parteiensystem im Wandel*, p. 9.

39. For copious evidence see Werner Kaltefleiter, *Wirtschaft und Politik in Deutschland. Konjunktur als Bestimmungsfaktor des Parteiensystems* (1966), 2nd edn, Cologne and Opladen, 1968. See also Hans Rattinger, *Wirtschaftliche Konjunktur und politische Wahlen in der Bundesrepublik Deutschland*, Berlin, 1980.

Table 4.5 West German results in the first three direct elections to the European Parliament, 1979–89

	1979		1984		1989	
	Votes %	Seats %	Votes %	Seats %	Votes %	Seats %
CDU/CSU	49.2	42	46.0	41	37.8	32
SPD	40.8	35	37.4	33	37.3	31
FDP	6.0	4	4.8	–	5.6	4
Die Grünen (The Greens)	3.2	–	8.2	–	8.4	8
Die Republikaner (The Republicans)	–	–	–	–	7.1	6
Deutsche Kommunistische Partei (German Communist Party)	0.4	–	–	–	0.1	–
National-Demokratische Partei Deutschlands (National Democratic Party of Germany)	–	–	0.4	–	–	–
Deutsche Volksunion (German People's Union)	–	–	–	–	1.6	–
Friedensliste (Peace List)	–	–	1.3	–	–	–
Ökologisch-Demokratische Partei (Ecological Democratic Party)	–	–	0.3	–	0.7	–
Others	0.4	–	1.6	–	1.4	–

Source: Emil Hübner and Horst Hennek Rohlfs, *Jahrbuch der Bundesrepublik Deutschland 1985/86*, Munich, 1985, p. 330; and *Jahrbuch der Bundesrepublik Deutschland 1989/90*, Munich, 1989, p. 239.

European elections   Since 1979 the European Parliament has been elected directly. Participation in the elections is low: in 1979 it was below 65%, in 1984 even lower, at 57%, at in 1989 round about 62%. Hence the turn-out is lower than that for local government elections. The reason may be a combination of 'European maturity' and 'European fatigue'. The term 'European maturity' means that citizens stay away from the elections because the European Parliament has inadequate powers: the elections, it is felt, have merely symbolic significance. The term 'European fatigue' indicates that in West Germany – and not only there – there is considerable disinterest in Europe. It is feared that one's own national interests are not sufficiently represented (for instance, in the area of agricultural policy). Typically, first-rate politicians are not sent to Strasbourg, especially as membership of the Bundestag excludes candidacy for the European Parliament. In the 1984 elections, all three parties formerly represented in the Parliament lost votes, because the Greens achieved a 5% increase and forced the FDP out (see Table 4.5). In 1989 the CDU/CSU lost over eight percentage points in overall support, while the Republicans, a party of the extreme right, won 7.1% of the vote and so gained entry to the Parliament. With the FDP regaining a presence, the number of German parties represented in the European Parliament increased to five. It should be noted that in the European elections the parties receive election-campaign reimbursements of DM 5 per citizen eligible to vote. These have often been used to cover debts, or in any case have not been used for the election campaign. It is high time that the law was changed so that the reimbursement relates only to voters.

In West Germany, European elections are seen as 'minor' elections with the following characteristics:[40] the election campaign is dominated by issues that the election is not really intended to air; the turn-out is considerably lower than for a 'major'; the voter is more inclined to give his vote to a smaller party, even though he knows that, by doing so, he is wasting his vote; and there is quite a definite pattern – immediately after a 'major' election the governing party may be successful in a European election, but later it loses a considerable number of votes, before eventually improving again. Of course, this is a generalisation, but it is true of European elections in many respects. For example, the 1979 and 1984 election campaigns were not primarily concerned with topics specific to Europe. Characteristically the CDU/CSU, as the opposition party, was by no means able to repeat in the 1980 Bundestag elections its

40. See Karlheinz Reif, 'Nationale Regierungsparteien verlieren die Wahl zum Europäischen Parlament 1984', *Zeitschrift für Parlamentsfragen*, 15/1984, pp. 341–52.

magnificent results in the 1979 European elections (49.2%) – not least because of the way the main candidates, Schmidt and Strauß, were viewed by the public.

Bundestag elections   To date, Bundestag elections have revealed impressive party stability. Changes have been limited, apart from during the early years before the party system was completely formed. When the CDU/CSU achieved an extremely narrow absolute majority of seats in the second Bundestag election, there was talk of an 'election miracle' (Dolf Sternberger). Since the 1961 elections, the highest difference from one election to the next has been 4.7% for the SPD (1983 losses against 1980) and 4.5% for the CDU/CSU (1987 losses against 1983). Between 1957 and 1972, the SPD continually increased its so-called 'comrade trend', whilst the CDU/CSU's proportion of the votes has oscillated between 44.3% (1987) and 50.2% (1957) since 1953.

Election results since 1949 reflect a high degree of party concentration (see Table 4.6). In the 1972 and 1976 Bundestag elections the CDU/CSU, SPD and FDP together achieved 99.1% of all votes. In the past few years, the degree of party concentration has declined, although it is still high compared with other European countries, so that there is currently little justification for the theory that the major parties' ability to attract and keep voters is threatened (even though election results are only *one* indicator of this) and that a process of deconcentration is occurring. It may be that in the next few years – as in other Western democracies – an extreme right-wing party will gain in popularity.[41]

In a sense, the West German party system is still labouring under the historical burden it carries. In the Bundestag, party concentration is intensified by the fact that votes for small parties which fail the 5% hurdle and do not succeed in winning seats benefit those parties already in the Bundestag. From 1961 to 1983 there were only three parliamentary parties, the CDU/CSU, the SPD and the FDP (see Table 4.7).

41. Claus Leggewie's informative observations in 'Die Zwerge am rechten Rand. Zu den Chancen kleiner neuer Rechtsparteien in der Bundesrepublik Deutschland', *Politische Vierteljahresschrift*, 28/1987, pp. 361–83.

Table 4.6 Distribution of second votes in Bundestag elections, 1949–87 (percentages)

Year	1949	1953	1957	1961	1965	1969	1972	1976	1980	1983	1987
Turn-out	78.5	86.0	87.0	87.7	86.8	86.7	91.1	90.7	88.6	89.1	84.3
CDU/CSU	31.0	45.2	50.2	45.3	47.6	46.1	44.9	48.6	44.5	48.8	44.3
SPD	29.2	28.8	31.8	36.2	39.3	42.7	45.8	42.6	42.9	38.2	37.0
FDP	11.9	9.5	7.7	12.8	9.5	5.8	8.4	7.9	10.6	7.0	9.1
Die Grünen	–	–	–	–	–	–	–	–	1.5	5.6	8.3
DP	4.0	3.3	3.4	–	–	–	–	–	–	–	–
BP	4.2	1.7	0.5	–	–	0.2	–	–	–	–	–
KPD	5.7	2.2	–	–	–	–	–	–	–	–	–
WAV	2.9	–	–	–	–	–	–	–	–	–	–
Zentrum	3.1	0.8	0.3	–	–	0.0	–	–	–	–	–
DReP	1.8	–	–	–	–	–	–	–	–	–	–
DRP	–	1.1	1.0	0.8	–	–	–	–	–	–	–
GB/BHE	–	5.9	4.6	–	–	–	–	–	–	–	–
GDP	–	–	–	2.8	–	–	–	–	–	–	–
DFU	–	–	–	1.9	1.3	0.1	–	–	–	–	–
NPD	–	–	–	–	2.0	4.3	0.6	0.3	0.2	0.2	0.6
DKP	–	–	–	–	–	–	0.3	0.3	0.2	0.2	–
Others	6.2	1.5	0.5	0.2	0.3	0.8	0.0	0.3	0.1	0.0	0.7

BP   Bayernpartei (Bavarian Party).
DFU   Deutsche Friedensunion (German Peace Union).
DKP   Deutsche Kommunistische Partei (German Communist Party).
DP   Deutsche Partei (German Party).
DReP   Deutsche Rechtspartei (German Justice Party).
DRP   Deutsche Reichspartei (German Reich Party).
GB/BHE   Gesamtdeutscher Block / Block der Heimatvertriebenen und Entrechteten (Pan-German Block / League of the Homeless and Dispossessed).
GDP   Gesamtdeutsche Partei (Pan-German Party).
KPD   Kommunistische Partei Deutschlands (Communist Party of Germany).
NPD   National-Demokratische Partei Deutschlands (National Democratic Party of Germany).
WAV   Wirtschaftliche Aufbauvereinigung (Industrial Construction Association).
Source: compiled from official statistics.

Table 4.7 Distribution of seats in the Bundestag 1949–87 (excluding Berlin MPs)

	1949	1953	1957	1961	1965	1969	1972	1976	1980	1983	1987
CDU	115	191	215	192	196	193	117	190	185	191	174
CSU	24	52	55	50	49	49	48	53	52	53	49
SPD	131	151	169	190	202	224	230	214	228	193	186
FDP	52	48	41	67	49	30	41	39	54	34	46
Die Grünen	–	–	–	–	–	–	–	–	–	27	42
DP	17	15	17	–	–	–	–	–	–	–	–
BP	17	–	–	–	–	–	–	–	–	–	–
KPD	15	–	–	–	–	–	–	–	–	–	–
WAV	12	–	–	–	–	–	–	–	–	–	–
Zentrum	10	3	–	–	–	–	–	–	–	–	–
DReP	5	–	–	–	–	–	–	–	–	–	–
Independents	3	–	–	–	–	–	–	–	–	–	–
SSW	1	–	–	–	–	–	–	–	–	–	–
GB/BHE	–	27	–	–	–	–	–	–	–	–	–

SSW Südschleswigsche Wählerverband (South Schleswig Voters' Union). For other minor parties, see the key to Table 4.6.
Source: compiled from West German statistical yearbooks. Figures apply to the start of each legislative period. Since 1949, the CDU and CSU have formed a permanent alliance.

Since 1953, apart from these parties, only two others have been able to overcome the 5% hurdle: the Gesamtdeutsche Block/Block der Heimatvertriebenen und Entrechteten (in 1953) and the Greens (Die Grünen, in 1983 and 1987). The stability of the party system is also reflected in the fact that premature elections have only taken place twice: in 1972 (because of a parliamentary stalemate after a failed vote of no confidence), and in 1983 (following a successful vote of no confidence).

Landtag elections   In accordance with the federal principle, elections must also take place in the Länder every four years (in North Rhine–Westphalia and in Saarland every five years). The electoral turn-out is on average 10% points below that of the Bundestag elections. There are Länder with a structural CDU/CSU majority and those with a structural SPD majority. Although it is something of a generalisation, one can say that the CDU/CSU is successful in the south, whilst the SPD is successful in the north, which is weaker structurally, although the north-south divide is by no means as pronounced as in Italy or Britain, for example. Nevertheless, the party-political majority in some Länder literally seems to be inherited: this is the case for the CSU in Bavaria, the CDU in Baden-Württemberg and Rhineland-Palatinate and for the SPD in Hamburg and Bremen. In other Länder, such as Lower Saxony, the party with the majority has changed frequently. The number of changes in government is modest. As a result of the change in Lower Saxony in 1976 under Albrecht, the CDU/CSU achieved a majority in the Bundesrat (the upper house of the West German parliament) and was able, if not to block, then at least to delay and modify partly the legislative programme of the SPD–FDP Federal government. In the 1980s there were a total of four changes of power: in 1981, owing to the 'Berlin corruption scandal', the SPD lost its Berlin majority and had to give way to a CDU minority government under Richard von Weizsäcker, which was later expanded into a CDU–FDP government; in 1985, the SPD under Oskar Lafontaine dissolved what had been the CDU–FDP government in Saarland; in 1987 the CDU, together with the FDP, was able to take over the government in Hessen after the first 'Red–Green' coalition at Land level had failed; and finally, in 1988, the CDU/CSU had to hand over the office of minister–president to the SPD in the Land where they are normally most successful, Schleswig-Holstein – an obvious reaction by the voters to the scandal surrounding the former minister–president, Uwe Barschel.

In electoral sociology, a subject of heated debate is the extent to which the Landtag elections are influenced by conditions at Federal level.[42] That there is a connection is in itself indisputable – only the question of weighting is controversial. The parties, who often involve Bundestag politicians in the Landtag election campaigns, tend to see the Landtag elections as a test for the Federal situation – but only if they are successful. If the reverse is true, they blame regional peculiarities. In fact, election-campaign topics are not confined to Land-specific affairs but also include Federal policy. This is partly because Land policy, owing to its low degree of publicity, is less suited to mobilising voters, especially as one can barely distinguish the effective differences between the parties. One cannot demand uniformity of living-conditions and at the same time express surprise that voting-behaviour in the Länder is strongly influenced by Federal policy issues.

The theory which characterises the Landtag elections as 'protest elections' has many points in its favour. The governing party in Bonn generally fares poorly in the Landtag elections, compared with the trend in Federal elections. Rainer Dinkel has examined this correlation for the period 1949–76. In sixty-five out of sixty-seven cases, the result achieved by the governing coalition was lower than its Federal trend.[43] This tendency has continued; it probably has less to do with lower election turn-outs than with floating voters who wish to transmit a warning to 'their' party. This has a serious effect, particularly in times of crisis. (The parallels with British by-elections are obvious, even if one must relativise the significance of the comparison, owing to bigger 'swings' in Britain.) However, one should not generalise

42. Particularly involved in this is Georg Fabritius: see his *Wechselwirkungen zwischen Landtagswahlen und Bundespolitik*, Meisenheim/Glan, 1978; 'Sind Landtagswahlen Bundesteilwahlen?', *Aus Politik Zeitgeschichte*, supplement to *Das Parlament*, B 21/1979, pp. 23–8; 'Landtagswahlen und Bundespolitik. Warum Landtagswahlen ohne bundespolitische Einflüsse und Auswirkungen undenkbar sind', in Wehling, *Westeuropas Parteiensystem im Wandel*, pp. 113–26.
43. See Reiner Dinkel, 'Der Zusammenhang zwischen Bundes- und Landtagswahlergebnissen', *Politische Vierteljahresschrift*, 18/1977, pp. 348–59.

the 'protest' character of these elections. While long-term changes usually become apparent first in Landtag elections, there are situations specific to each Land which must be considered separately from Federal trends. All four changes of Land government in the 1980s were based on issues specific to the individual Länder. This is particularly true of the Landtag elections in Schleswig-Holstein in May 1988, which were affected by the wheelings and dealings of the former CDU minister–president Uwe Barschel. The CDU/CSU's losses were exclusively 'home-made'. The change of power in Hessen in 1987 was unique: for the first time in the history of the Federal Republic, the governing party in Bonn achieved victory in a Land where it had previously been in opposition.

To date, Bundestag and Landtag elections have occurred at the same time on only one occasion. A comparision of the results of this double election on 6 March 1983 (when the Bundestag elections occurred at the same time as the Landtag elections in Rhineland–Palatinate) is rendered more difficult by the fact that there is a single-vote system for the Land elections, but a two-vote system for Bundestag elections. If one assumes that opposing voter movements which would balance themselves out again in the final result do not exist, and that the Bundestag vote prejudices the Landtag vote, there were almost no differences between Landtag and Bundestag election results (when comparing with the Bundestag, one must admittedly consider the first votes, because obviously some 'true' CDU/CSU voters voted for the FDP with their second vote). If Landtag and Bundestag elections were regularly held at the same time, as is occasionally suggested, the significance of the Landtag elections would be further undermined, and thus this suggestion holds no attraction for supporters of federalism.

The Länder, where there were a number of all-party governments and Grand Coalitions in the initial phases of the Federal Republic, also serve as a 'testing-ground' for the parliamentary system. In the Länder – with a few exceptions – the same coalition patterns are formed as at Federal level. No party has participated as frequently in coalitions as the FDP.[44] Often,

44. For details, see Peter Haungs, 'Koalitionen und Koalitionsstrategien in der Bundesrepublik. Geschichte und Systematik', in Wehling, *Westeuropas Parteiensystem im Wandel*, pp. 95–112.

certain tendencies towards change initially appear at Land level, and are later expressed at Federal level.

It is often said that there is little point in having a parliamentary system of government for the Länder, in view of the limited powers that they possess. Critics suggest that all major parties should participate in the Land government in proportion to their percentage of votes at Federal level. Admittedly, since the 1950s, powers of jurisdiction in numerous areas have shifted from the Länder to the Bundestag, but bureaucratic pressures do not always override political decisions taken in the Land parliaments. This makes it possible to implement reforms without entailing major risks. For this reason and others it would not be appropriate to abolish the parliamentary system of government in the Länder, and, anyway, the subject is not really on the agenda.

Local government elections   According to article 28, paragraph 1, of the Basic Law, the people must be represented not only at Federal and Land level but also in the districts and counties. Depending on the Land, local government elections occur every four to six years; different local constitutional systems apply (the North German Constitution; municipal-authority constitution; South German Constitution; mayoral constitution).[45] Elements of Federal policy are much less important in local government elections than in European and Landtag elections. In view of their subordinate significance, then, they are not 'test elections'. This is shown by, for example, the low turn-out, which on average (although there are upswings and downswings) is a further 10% below that for Landtag elections. However, this does not alter the fact that the parties predominate, although admittedly in those Länder where the Bürgermeister is directly elected (Bavaria, Baden-Württemberg) the role of the parties is somewhat less significant, owing to the existence of so-called 'free voters' associations' (political interest groups which do not have the same official status as parties), and there is some emphasis on voting for an individual rather than a party (within

45. See (though now somewhat out of date) Dieter Nohlen, 'Wahlsysteme und Wahlen in den Gemeinden', in Heinz Rausch and Theo Stammen (eds), *Aspekte und Probleme der Kommunalpolitik*, Munich, 1973, pp. 151–85.

the proportional representation system).[46] The voters' associations, which have come to represent considerable competition to the FDP in particular, campaign exclusively in the parishes and justify this with the argument that a politicalisation of local government activities is not desirable, especially as a lack of 'closeness to the people' is often apparent among politicians. This view has some validity (although local government administration can never be completely 'apolitical') but it does run the risk of encouraging political neutrality, especially as the 'town hall parties' capitalise on the electorate's antipathy to the major parties to win votes for themselves.

Unlike in the Bundestag and Landtag elections, in local government elections there is often no unified trend, although from time to time certain tendencies emerge – for instance, in large cities – that later become apparent in other elections. To date, electoral sociology has paid little attention to this area.[47] The fact that results differ from those in Bundestag elections is partly interpreted as reflecting the low turn-out (which is disadvantageous to the governing party in Bonn), and partly explained in terms of factors specific to the region (for instance, the personalities involved). The following statement is perhaps a little rash:

> The new party groupings which exist at local level are a logical expression of multifarious changes in orientation or of a new orientation towards problems in the areas of ecology, the social environment and the economy, which is also the expression of a general reluctance as far as politics, or more precisely the state, is concerned.[48]

Much depends on whether 'green' or 'alternative' groups can be successful in local government in the long term. The 'free voters' associations' are recruited mainly from among local dignitaries, despite the fact that the 'green/alternative' milieu has its roots in the districts.

46. See for example the interesting case studies in Berthold Löffler and Walter Rogg, 'Determinanten kommunalen Wahlverhaltens in Baden-Württemberg. Dargestellt am Beispiel der Stadt Ravensburg', dissertation, Tübingen, 1985, esp. pp. 473–80.
47. One exception is Institut für Kommunalwissenschaften der Konrad-Adenauer-Stiftung (ed.), *Kommunales Wahlverhalten*, Bonn, 1976.
48. Heinz Zielinski, 'Wahlverhalten (WVh.) in Kommunalwahlen (KW)', in Rüdiger Voigt (ed.), *Handwörterbuch der Kommunalpolitik*, Opladen, 1984, p. 498.

As the above comparisons show, voting-behaviour is much the same in all elections (although to the least extent in local government elections). This is an indication of the constancy of the party system and voting-behaviour. However, it would be wrong to assume that the citizen must limit his political activities to the act of voting in 'major' and 'minor' elections. Active membership in parties, freedom of association (for instance, citizens' initiatives) and freedom of assembly (for example, in demonstrations) contradict such an assumption. If one considers all three 'fields' of political participation, one could even speak, albeit somewhat audaciously, of a 'participatory revolution' (Max Kaase).

Conclusion: Is There an Alternative to Elections?

Party democracy, with its (admittedly acyclical) changes of government and opposition, has proved itself full of vitality. The 'demise of the parties' predicted by Krippendorff and others has still not occurred. This is shown not only by developments in the Western states but also (for example) by those in Eastern Europe or in developing dictatorships in the Third World. Demands for opposition and for democratic elections have not fallen silent.

It is a fallacy to claim that those who are strongly in favour of the representation model, which does not necessarily exclude co-determination in other areas of society, are 'elitist', whilst advocates of an ideology which prophesies doom for the 'depoliticised' and demands 'true people's power' are promoting participation. Representative democracy, based on the competitive theory of democracy, comprising periodic elections and a number of further opportunities for participation, does not lead to the electorate becoming impotent, because the intermediary powers, for reasons of self-interest, are aware of the law of 'anticipated reaction'. Note that, in this concept, the intermediary powers are considered not only legitimate, but also essential. This model of democracy leaves room for leadership, guarantees the protection of minorities, and ensures a high degree of liberality. Of course, forms of structure vary. Whilst most forms of participation are limited primarily to the act of voting, there are those who argue that other forms of political participation are necessary to prevent the power structures from becoming crystallised, encrusted, petrified or fossilised, to use a few new-fangled words.

> If one wants minority rule as well as minority protection, participation as well as leadership, social and political equality as well as individual freedom, there is no recognisable political structure which

does justice to this request other than the representative system of Western democracy. This is not least related to the opportunity for and promotion of social change, which is supported as far as possible by consensus.[1]

But representative democracy, in which elections (and not referenda) form the decisive element, is for ever being confronted with the same accusations: 'second-best solution', 'emergency solution', 'temporary measure', 'deficient form of democracy', 'incomplete democracy', 'pale copy of true democracy'.[2] In fact it would be a weak argument to try to justify representative democracy by saying that direct democracy is not possible in a mass democracy. Such an assumption would entail equating democracy with 'self-determination' and would necessitate cutbacks in the democratic constitutional state (which would be expressed in the aforementioned characteristics). The democratic constitutional state represents a complicated synthesis of the principle of democracy and the principle of office.[3]

The two principles are not easily reconciled, but they are nevertheless . . . dependent on one another: only by fusing them together can there be a legitimate, free state. The principle of democracy promises every citizen the same right to free participation and co-determination in common issues, and condenses these rights to the concept of people's sovereignty. The principle of office states that all authority to make binding decisions for others should be drawn up as an office.[4]

The authorised holder of an office, who holds his position on the condition that he may be removed from office, must

1. Wolfgang Jäger, 'Prämissen der repräsentativen Demokratie', in Dieter Oberndörfer and Wolfgang Jäger (eds), *Die neue Elite*, Freiburg/Breisgau, 1975, p. 66.
2. These accusations are listed (and convincingly refuted) in Peter Graf Kielmansegg, '"Die Quadratur des Zirkels". Überlegungen zum Charakter der repräsentativen Demokratie', in Ulrich Matz (ed.), *Aktuelle Herausforderungen der repräsentativen Demokratie*, Cologne, 1985, pp. 9–41 (quotations p. 9f.)
3. See Wilhelm Hennis, 'Amtsgedanke und Demokratiebegriff' (1962), in Joseph A. Schumpeter, *Die mißverstandene Demokratie. Demokratie–Verfassung– Parlament. Studien zu deutschen Problemen*, Freiburg/Breisgau, 1973, pp. 9–25, pp. 144–7.
4. Graf Kielmansegg, in Matz, *Aktuelle Herausforderungen*, p. 22.

direct himself towards the common weal when making decisions on behalf of other people. Hence it is inadequate to consider the human right to self-determination without examining also the extent to which this is bound up in the mechanism of the system of office-holding. However, this also means that the supporter of representative democracy should be the first to object to any misuse of the principle of office, as occurred in Schleswig-Holstein in 1987 in such an unusual way that representative democracy suffered heavy damage.

By agreeing with Karl R. Popper in rejecting any form of historicism, one is assuming the openness of any future political events and hence expressing scepticism towards any form of historical determinism. The overview given in this book, however, is intended to show that there 'is currently no other system which is able to focus unrest and at the same time convert it into positive new policies as successfully as parliamentary democracy can'.[5]

Against this background, the dispute regarding the relative merits of proportional representation and the majority system is not of essential significance, although in the past, particularly in West Germany, this dispute has been conducted extremely passionately. It would also be wrong to make the sweeping accusation that, because of its scientific approach to the subject, electoral research makes no contribution to democracy. Electoral research helps to strengthen democracy *per se*, because it is concerned with an area of political life which is an important characteristic of democracy and helps develop it further.

Sporadic attempts to develop an alternative to elections are hardly convincing. This is also true of the following suggestions – one 'moderate' and one 'radical'. The 'moderate' proposal involves criticism of the majority principle, and the 'radical' proposal is concerned with the abolition of elections.

In recent years there has been increasing criticism of parliamentary democracy based on majority rule.[6] The general line

---

5. Klaus von Beyme, 'Die Zukunft der parlamentarischen Demokratie', in Klaus von Beyme, Ernst-Otto Czempiel, Peter Graf Kielmansegg and Peter Schmoock (eds), *Politikwissenschaft. Eine Grundlegung*, vol. 2: *Der demokratische Verfassungsstaat*, Stuttgart, 1987, p. 332.

6. See for example Bernd Guggenberger and Claus Offe (eds), *An den Grenzen der Mehrheitsdemokratie. Politik und Soziologie der Mehrheitsregel*, Opladen, 1984.

of criticism is that, following some irreversible and highly controversial decisions, majority rule is no longer able to fulfil a pacifying function. Highly motivated minorities are not adequately represented. People who play off 'apathetic, ill-informed majorities who are completely disinterested because they themselves are not personally affected' against 'involved, well-informed and highly affected minorities'[7] are compromising the majority principle, which is based on the principle of equal elections. In fact, recognition of this principle does involve making some assumptions. It can only develop its legitimising effect by leaving important basic values untouched. However, value-bound democracy is based on the very fact that these principles are steadfast in their application. Criticism of the majority principle, although this is much disputed, in the end amounts to little more than playing down the relevance of the act of voting.

A more radical type of criticism has recently been expressed by John Burnheim, who sees himself as representing neither a right-wing extremist movement nor a left-wing one. He totally rejects elections because they are 'detrimental to rule by and for the people'.[8] Some of the points he makes are similar to the criticisms aimed at 'majority democracy' – for example, the argument that the intensity of a decision is not expressed in the act of voting:

> A majority which only has slight preferences in one direction can outvote nearly the same number of strong preferences in the opposing direction. In addition, referenda usually involve entire presentation packages, which are either swallowed as a whole or rejected, so that we necessarily betray many of our wishes, whatever decision we make. The reason why referenda are so insignificant is that they register such an extremely small amount of information.[9]

For a criticism see Heinrich Oberreuter (ed.), *Wahrheit statt Mehrheit? An den Grenzen der parlamentarischen Demokratie*, Munich, 1986; Hans Hattenhauer and Werner Kaltefleiter (eds), *Mehrheitsprinzip, Konsens und Verfassung*, Heidelberg, 1986.

7. Bernd Guggenberger, 'An den Grenzen der Mehrheitsdemokratie', in Guggenberger and Offe, *An den Grenzen der Mehrheitsdemokratie*, p. 191.

8. John Burnheim, *Über Demokratie. Alternativen zum Parlamentarismus*, Berlin, 1987, p. 95.

9. Ibid., p. 96.

State powers, Burnheim argues, should be decentralised and divided into different functional units, which he does not envisage any serious problems in co-ordinating. Burnheim believes that political offices should be distributed by drawing lots so that people cannot make careers out of politics, especially as it is envisaged that people will swap offices. His alternative to a parliamentary democracy based on elections is termed *Démarchie*. He claims that it could be gradually introduced into highly industrialised countries where there is time for public discussion and decision-making.

One certainly does not wish to reject unconventional ideas as taboo or even to denounce them as anti-democratic without analysing and evaluating their contents. But, seen in the cold light of day, Burnheim's proposal is naïve, unrealistic and certainly not suitable for a society based on the principle of the division of labour, which requires experts. Drawing lots only serves to encourage incompetence; deprofessionalisation must necessarily lead to excessive demands being made on the decision-makers; the principle of responsibility is inadequately implemented, because the political authorities cannot be called to account; and, furthermore, Burnheim's suggestion, although he does not actually say so, is based on an enormous faith in mankind. The dangers inherent in such a model without elections are obvious.

Elections – is there an alternative? This question is a rhetorical one, as was the question posed by Wilhelm Grewe in 1951 – 'Parties – is there an alternative?'[10] – and Carl Schmitt's question, 'Parliamentarism, is there an alternative?' If one dismisses this question, as Schmitt did, as a 'helpless argument',[11] one deserves to be told that the onus for proposing a new process lies with the critics. Otherwise, it would be all too easy to express criticisms aimed at destroying what already exists without offering a solution. Only the election process allows a government to be dissolved peacefully. In this sense, it is an instrument that is both legitimate and effective.

10. Cf. Wilhelm Grewe, 'Parteienstaat – oder was sonst?', *Der Monat*, 3.36/ 1950–1, pp. 563–77.
11. Carl Schmitt, *Die geistesgeschichtliche Lage des heutigen Parlamentarismus* (1923), 4th edn, Berlin, 1969, p. 90.

Annotated Bibliography

Bogdanor, Vernon (ed.), *Representatives of the People? Parliamentarians and Constituents in Western Democracies*, Aldershot: Gower, 1985, 310 pages. The essays in this book examine an area which is often neglected: the question of how well elections in Western democracies guarantee a connection between the electorate and those elected.

Bogdanor, Vernon, and David Butler (eds), *Democracy and Elections: Electoral Systems and their Political Consequences*, Cambridge: Cambridge University Press, 1983, 267 pages. Systematically examines electoral and party systems in Western countries. The essays, as in the preceding reader, are supplemented by an introduction and summary by Bogdanor.

Bürklin, Wilhelm, *Wählerverhalten und Wertewandel*, Opladen: Leske Verlag und Budrich, 1988, 144 pages. A succinct overview of empirical electoral research with particular attention to theoretical concepts and the change in values. The author provides the foundations of a theory of voting-behaviour.

Büsch, Otto (ed.), *Wählerbewegung in der europäischen Geschichte. Ergebnisse einer Konferenz*, Berlin: Colloquium Verlag, 1980, 579 pages. This anthology is not only useful for teaching-purposes, but should also act as an incentive to 'pay more attention to the electoral fluctuations as one of the most significant historical forces of the 19th and 20th century'.

Büsch, Otto and Peter Steinbach (eds), *Vergleichende europäische Wahlgeschichte. Eine Anthologie. Beiträge zur historischen Wahlforschung vornehmlich West- und Nordeuropas*, Berlin: Colloquium Verlag, 1983, 503 pages. Important contributions on historical electoral research, particularly on the history of the European election.

Burnheim, John, *Über Demokratie. Alternativen zum Parlamentarismus*, Berlin: Verlag Klaus Wagenbach, 1987, 191 pages. The author develops a provocative alternative to representative democracy: the so-called *Démarchie*, based on a system of drawing lots. It involves a 'network of decentralised bodies', 'in which individual interests are articulated on the spot'.

113

Falter, Jürgen, Thomas Lindenberger and Siegfried Schumann, *Wahlen und Abstimmungen in der Weimarer Republic. Materialien zum Wahlverhalten 1919–1933*, Munich: Verlag C. H. Beck, 1986, 251 pages. Very well-documented statistical workbook on elections in the first German democracy. The book expresses opinions about voter movements which are based on some complicated calculations, particularly in relation to the $64,000 question 'Who voted for Hitler?'

Fenske, Hans, *Strukturprobleme der deutschen Parteiengeschichte. Wahlrecht und Parteiensystem vom Vormärz bis heute*, Frankfurt/Main: Athenäum Verlag, 1974, 230 pages. This shortened version of a post-doctoral thesis examines the changing relationships between the electoral system and the development of the German party system, with particular attention to the Weimar Republic. Fenske's basic theory is that the individual electoral system has only minimal influence on the formation of the party system.

Graf, Herbert and Günther Seiler, *Wahl und Wahlrecht im Klassenkampf*, Berlin (East): Staatsverlag der Deutschen Demokratischen Republik, 1971, 441 pages. Study of the role of elections from a Marxist–Leninist point of view. The basic theory is as follows: 'Elections and voting are primarily influenced by the class character of the social order in which they occur . . . and in particular by the demands made by the class struggle in that particular historical period.'

Grofman, Bernard and Arend Lijphart (eds), *Electoral Laws and their Political Consequences*, New York: Agathon Press, 1986, 335 pages. This anthology analyses in particular the influence of voting-conditions on the characteristics of the party system.

Henkel, Joachim, *Die Auswahl der Parlamentsbewerber. Grundfragen–Verfahrensmodell*, Berlin and New York: Verlag Walter de Gruyter, 1976, 335 pages. Informative analysis of the selection of constituency and list candidates for the Bundestag, with particular emphasis on the proposals which have been made for increasing the rights of both 'ordinary voters' and 'party voters'.

Hermens, Ferdinand A., *Demokratie oder Anarchie? Untersuchung über die Verhältniswahl* (1941), 2nd edn, Cologne: Westdeutscher Verlag, 1968, 346 pages. The founder of the 'Cologne School', whose life's work has been concerned with the demise of the first German democracy, sees proportional representation as the root of all evils. A 'classical' work in defence of the majority system.

Hofmann-Göttig, Joachim, *Die jungen Wähler. Zur Interpretation der Jungwählerdaten der 'Repräsentativen Wahlstatistik' für Bundestag, Landtag und Europaparlament 1953–1984*, Frankfurt/Main: Campus Verlag, 1984, 174 pages. The author interprets the voting-behaviour of young voters from an analysis of the official representative election statistics. The material he presents here is a real treasure trove.

Hofmann-Göttig, Joachim, *Emanzipation mit dem Stimmzettel. 70 Jahre Frauenwahlrecht in Deutschland*, Bonn: Verlag Neue Gesellschaft, 1986, 143 pages. This study is also based on official statistics. Its main finding is that the SPD no longer suffers from a 'deficit of women'.

Hübner, Emil, *Wahlsysteme und ihre möglichen Wirkungen unter spezieller Berücksichtigung der Bundesrepublik Deutschland*, 6th edn, Munich: Bayerische Landeszentrale für politische Bildungsarbeit, 1984, 240 pages. The author, who presents reliable information regarding different forms of electoral systems and their advantages and disadvantages, provides a particularly useful analysis of the debate on voting-rights in West Germany.

Institut für Kommunalwisssenschaften der Konrad-Adenauer-Stiftung, *Kommunales Wahlverhalten*, Bonn: Eichholz Verlag, 1976, 308 pages. A project group (Franz Urban Pappi, Klaus Simon, Klaus-Dieter Hartmann, Hans-Dieter Klingemann, Paul Kevenhörster) examines an area previously unresearched – the factors which determine local government voting-behaviour.

Jesse, Eckhard, *Wahlrecht zwischen Kontinuität und Reform. Eine Analyse der Wahlsystemdiskussion und der Wahlrechtsänderungen in der Bundesrepublik Deutschland 1949–1983*, Düsseldorf: Droste Verlag, 1985, 440 pages. Summary of the debates surrounding the electoral system and evaluation of changes in voting-rights (e.g. the 5% hurdle and the two-vote system). The book contains extensive statistical material on the history of elections in West Germany.

Kaase, Max and Hans-Dieter Klingemann (eds), *Wahlen und politisches System. Analysen aus Anlaß der Bundestagswahl 1980*, Opladen: Westdeutscher Verlag, 1983, 651 pages. Comprehensive book containing research into voting-behaviour in the 1980 Bundestag elections. Considers the role played by both the mass media and economic development.

Kaltefleiter, Werner and Peter Nißen, *Empirische Wahlforschung. Eine*

Einführung in Theorie und Technik, Paderborn: Schöningh Verlag, 1980, 224 pages. 'Electoral research is one of those areas of research which have only recently been developed but which nevertheless receive great attention from the public, who view it with a mixture of high hopes and deep-rooted scepticism.' This book, which is aimed at a specific target group, sets out to prove that neither of these attitudes is justified.

Klingemann, Hans-Dieter and Max Kaase (eds), *Wahlen und politischer Prozeß. Analysen aus Anlaß der Bundestagswahl 1983*, Opladen: Westdeutscher Verlag, 1986, 543 pages. This book is the latest in a series on Bundestag elections, prepared under the aegis of the experts on electoral research, Kaase and Klingemann, and already something of a classic. Unfortunately, the books appeared only shortly before the following Bundestag elections.

Kort-Krieger, Ute and Jörn W. Mundt, *Praxis der Wahlforschung. Eine Einführung*, Frankfurt/Main and New York, Campus Verlag, 1986, 224 pages. Textbook giving an overview of voting-behaviour. The book also contains didactically prepared data on Bundestag elections from 1961 to 1983.

Lange, Erhard H. M., *Wahlrecht und Innenpolitik. Entstehungsgeschichte und Analyse der Wahlgesetzgebung und Wahlrechtsdiskussion im westlichen Nachkriegsdeutschland 1945–1956*, Meisenheim/Glan: Anton Hain Verlag, 1975, 883 pages. Standard work regarding the structure of voting-rights in West Germany up till the 1956 ruling. The author concentrates mainly on party interests and politicians' motives, which are based largely on power politics.

Lapp, Peter J., *Wahlen in der DDR. Wählt die Kandidaten der Nationalen Front!*, Berlin: Verlag Gebr. Holzapfel, 1982, 138 pages. Succinct introductory work on elections in the other German state. Informative appendix.

Lijphart, Arendt and Bernard Grofman (eds), *Choosing an Electoral System: Issues and Alternatives*, New York: Praeger, 1984, 273 pages. Analysis of the problems surrounding electoral systems in various countries. Various 'old masters' of research into electoral systems are quoted: Maurice Duverger, George H. Hallett Jr, Ferdinand A. Hermens, Enid Lakeman. Indispensable work for comparative research.

Ménudier, Henri, *Les Elections allemandes 1969–1982*, Paris and Strasbourg: Centre d'Information et de Recherche sur l'Allemagne Contemporaine, 1982, 416 pages. One of the best French experts on Germany presents an analysis of Bundestag and Landtag elections during the SPD-FDP coalition.

Meyer, Hans, *Wahlsystem und Verfassungsordnung: Bedeutung und Grenzen wahlsystematischer Gestaltung nach dem Grundgesetz*, Frankfurt/Main: Alfred Metzner Verlag, 1973, 300 pages. Pioneering work on the classification of electoral systems, developing of the concept of a continuum. The author considers proportional representation to be the appropriate electoral system for parliamentary democracy.

Mielke, Gerd, *Sozialer Wandel und politische Dominanz in Baden-Württemberg. Eine politikwissenschaftlich-statistische Analyse des Zusammenhangs von Sozialstruktur und Wahlverhalten in einer ländlichen Region*, Berlin: Verlag Duncker und Humblot, 1987, 337 pages. New and commendable example of a study of regional elections. Voting-behaviour from 1960 to 1976 is systematically examined in one of the CDU's 'stronghold' Länder.

Nohlen, Dieter, *Wahlsysteme der Welt. Daten und Analysen. Ein Handbuch*, Munich: R. Piper Verlag, 1978, 449 pages. The handbook, which combines theoretical problems with empirical analyses, gives a systematic, basic overview of all 'electoral systems in the world'. Indispensable for research into electoral systems.

Nohlen, Dieter, *Wahlrecht und Parteiensystem*, Opladen: Leske Verlag und Budrich, Opladen 1986, 248 pages. The author, who has long been familiar with the available material on voting, analyses the electoral systems of various countries (in addition to West Germany, he also pays particular attention to Britain, France, Spain and Ireland) and discusses the question of whether and to what extent the individual electoral systems are reponsible for forming the party system.

Oberndörfer, Dieter, Hans Rattinger and Karl Schmitt (eds), *Wirtschaftlicher Wandel, religiöser Wandel und Wertwandel. Folgen für das politische Verhalten in der Bundesrepublik*, Berlin: Verlag Duncker und Humblot, 1985, 412 pages. Excellent reader with new empirical material on the economic and religious changes in West Germany, as well as the changes in values, in relation to the changes in voting-behaviour.

Ritter, Gerhard A. and Merith Niehuss, *Wahlen in der Bundesrepublik Deutschland. Bundestags- und Landtagswahlen 1946–1987*, 228 pages. The CDU election campaign manager writes: 'Modern election campaigning as a form of political communication is the explosive mixture of political events and advertising campaigns, of political topics, personalities and advertising messages.'

Rohe, Karl (ed.), *Elections, Parties and Political Traditions: Social Foundations of German Parties and Party Systems, 1867–1987*, Oxford: Berg Publishers, 1990, 256 pages. This collection looks at German parties and party systems at regional level and in historical perspective. Supplemented by an extensive Bibliography.

Rose, Richard (ed.), *Electoral Behaviour: A Comparative Handbook*, London: Collier-Macmillan, 1974, 753 pages. Comprehensive analysis of elections in Western democracies on a comparative basis. A follow-up volume for the 1970s and 1980s would be useful.

Schmitt, Karl, *Konfession und Wahlverhalten in der Bundesrepublik Deutschland*, Berlin: Verlag Duncker und Humblot, 1990, 440 pages. This study, which was originally a post-doctoral thesis, examines the development of voting-behaviour which is determined by religious considerations, together with the reasons for this. The basic argument is that the role of religion in voting-behaviour must not be underestimated, despite the process of secularisation which has occurred.

Schreiber, Wolfgang, *Handbuch des Wahlrechts zum Deutschen Bundestag. Kommentar zum Bundeswahlgesetz unter Einbeziehung der Bundeswahlordnung, der Bundeswahlgeräteverordnung und sonstiger wahlrechtlicher Nebenvorschriften*, 3rd edn, Cologne: Carl Heymanns Verlag, 1986, 756 pages. Schreiber is the standard commentator on Federal electoral law. The most recent edition examines changes in Federal electoral law since 1985.

Sternberger, Dolf, *Die große Wahlreform. Zeugnisse einer Bemühung*, Opladen: Westdeutscher Verlag, 1964, 251 pages. These essays by the founder of the 'Heidelberg School', in favour of a majority electoral system, are also testimony to the failure of 'the major electoral reform' to materialise.

Sternberger, Dolf and Bernhard Vogel (eds), *Die Wahl der Parlamente und anderer Staatsorgane. Ein Handbuch*, vol. 1: *Europa*, Berlin: Walter de Gruyter Verlag, 1969, 1489 pages. This book, edited by Dieter Nohlen, replaced the 1932 'Braunias'. The development of the franchise and voting-behaviour is examined separately for each country in a historical, systematic manner.

Vogel, Bernhard, Dieter Nohlen and Rainer-Olaf Schultze, *Wahlen in Deutschland. Theorie–Geschichte–Dokumente 1848–1970*, Berlin: Walter de Gruyter Verlag, 1971, 465 pages. This study is based mainly on the handbook *Die Wahl der Parlamente und anderer Staatsorgane*. A good overview of 'conceptual bases' and 'history of elections in Germany'.

Vring, Thomas von der, *Reform oder Manipulation? Zur Diskussion eines neuen Wahlrechts*, Frankfurt/Main: Europäische Verlagsanstalt, 1968, 313 pages. A polemical work in defence of the system of proportional representation – a subject which is no longer topical, in West Germany at least.

Wahlatlas 1987/88 Bundesrepublik Deutschland. 60 Kapitel von 1949 bis 1987. Karten und Kommentare, 3rd edn, Brunswick: Verlag Höller und Zwick, 1988, 211 pages. Documentation of all Bundestag, European, President and Chancellor elections in West Germany, together with the most recent Landtag and local government elections. Ideal for political studies; excellent graphic illustrations.

Wahlatlas Europa. Wahlen und Abstimmungen in allen Mitgliedstaaten der Europäischen Gemeinschaft, Brunswick: Verlag Höller und Zwick, 1988, 163 pages. Similar structure to the above. The book, which is likewise well-illustrated, examines the results of the parliamentary elections in all EC states as well as those of national referenda.

Wehling, Hans-Georg (ed.), *Westeuropas Parteiensystem im Wandel*, Stuttgart: Kohlhammer Verlag, 1983, 198 pages. Excellent anthology of problem-oriented contributions on West Germany and on the party system in other Western democracies (France, Italy, Spain, Britain).

Wolf, Werner, *Wahlkampf und Demokratie*, Cologne: Verlag Wissenschaft und Politik, 1985, 151 pages. The author, who attempts to demythologise what are frequently complicated election campaigns, analyses the role and function of election campaigns and party strategies.

Woyke, Wichard and Udo Steffens, *Stichwort Wahlen. Ein Ratgeber für Wähler und Kandidaten*, 6th edn, Opladen: Leske Verlag und Budrich, 1990, 204 pages. This book is useful for political studies. As the title suggests, it examines electoral problems by utilising key terms.